MY GAY HUSBAND

How my gay ex-husband became my best friend

LEANNE AZZOPARDI

ABOUT THE AUTHOR

Leanne Azzopardi is a Melbourne-based teacher, writer and mother to three young adults. *My Gay Husband* is her first published book, although she has written her mother's memoir for her extended family. Since 2004, Leanne has assisted children with disabilities, particularly those with Autism Spectrum Disorder. Her career arose from helping a family member, who was diagnosed with mild Autism when he was three years old. She also works as a tutor in mathematics and is avidly interested in genealogy. Her interests include writing poetry, song lyrics, music and staying healthy by working out at the gym.

Published in Australia by Sid Harta Publishers Pty Ltd.
ABN: 34 632 585 203
17 Coleman Parade, GLEN WAVERLEY VIC 3150 Australia
Telephone: +61 3 9560 9920, Facsimile: +61 3 9545 1742
E-mail: author@sidharta.com.au

First published in Australia 2019
This edition published 2019
Copyright © Leanne Azzopardi 2019
Cover design, typesetting: WorkingType (www.workingtype.com.au)

The right of Leanne Azzopardi to be identified as the Author of the Work has been asserted in accordance with the Copyright, Designs and Patents Act 1988.

The Author of this book accepts all responsibility for the contents and absolves any other person or persons involved in its production from any responsibility or liability where the contents are concerned.

All rights reserved. No part of this publication may be reproduced, stored in a retrieval system, or transmitted, in any form or by any means without the prior written permission of the publisher, nor be otherwise circulated in any form of binding or cover other than that in which it is published and without a similar condition being imposed on the subsequent purchaser.

Azzopardi, Leanne
My Gay Husband
ISBN: 978-1-925230-73-4
pp170

My Gay Husband is dedicated to anyone who has experienced the heartache of a marriage break-up, particularly when one partner has concealed their sexual preferences. My book was at times harrowing to write, yet somehow cathartic. My story is one of recovery and healing from the rollercoaster of emotions that ranged from feeling betrayed, to having a damaged self-esteem. I hope that readers will gain courage in knowing that life can get better, even when it feels as though your world is shattered. My wish is that everyone is true to their own sexual identity and to those they love.

Special thanks to my three children, Brandon, Sarah and Charlotte. You are my love, my strength and light. To my dear sisters and close friends, thank you for your support and for being my survival kit. To Julian, thank you for the friendship that survived the ashes of our marriage. Finally, a wholehearted thanks to Sid Harta Publishers for believing in the true story that must be told.

PREFACE

I am truly grateful to all who have supported me throughout both the positive and the most challenging parts of my life. Without you I would never be in the position to put pen to paper. You are my strength and my light. For their love and patience, I would like to thank my three children, my sisters, friends and colleagues.

My goal in writing this book is to give hope to those who experience the heartache of a marriage break up, including the children involved. I also hope that by telling my story, other men and women will think twice before making a commitment to someone on false pretences, whether they are concealing their sexual identity or for any other reason. There are no winners in this situation, just further challenges that no one ever wants to face. Be true to yourself and you will have peace.

How my gay ex-husband became my best friend…

CHAPTER 1

It is perplexing to know where to begin a memoir, especially when the story is so close to home and taking place at this very minute. When I think back to certain events, I feel the tears well in my eyes, remembering a time when my life began to change in so many ways. Often, curve balls are thrown at most of us in many shapes and forms but nothing on this Earth could have prepared me for this one. It was the year of my fiftieth birthday, half a century old, a time when many couples are contemplating retirement and looking forward to spending precious holidays together. At least that is how I imagined my life would be. However, fate had other plans. A transformation I could never expect or would ever choose.

This excruciatingly painful, rollercoaster ride first

began on a hot, humid summer evening on the fourth of January 2016. It is funny how some dates and events just stay in your mind, like an indelible ink stain, never to be removed, just fading slightly over time. On this night, I was feeling extremely fatigued, which was nothing out of the ordinary for me, so I went to bed thinking I would sleep as soon as my head hit the pillow and not read my novel as I nearly always did. I loved to read as I found it relaxing and comforting. I read anything I could get my hands on, whether it was fiction, non-fiction or occasionally a trashy magazine. It was nearly 11pm on my alarm clock. I brushed my teeth thoroughly and briskly changed into my favourite pink, bunny rabbit pyjamas, proceeding to crawl into bed. I fluffed up my pillows and turned down the doona. Usually by now my husband, Julian, would be snoring his head off like a chainsaw in full flight, but that night it was different. He was sitting up in bed, wearing his Western Bulldogs boxers and white singlet, revealing his freshly shaved chest.

I looked up at the family photo of the five of us above our bed, promising myself to dust it tomorrow when I had a spare moment. Julian's bald head was shining brightly under the bed lamp, his big dark eyes expressionless, like he was trying to solve a complex puzzle. He appeared to have something on his mind, staring absorbedly at the cream coloured walls of our

CHAPTER 1

bedroom, as if he were watching a tear-jerking movie. I was ready to say 'Good night' to Julian, reaching over to receive the familiar, customary peck, when he handed me a plain white envelope with my name on the front. It did not feel like a card or a gift, so I was baffled as to what this could be.

'What's this?' I asked.

At that moment, Julian appeared mute, a tear running down his cheek and unable to speak a word. He started to sob uncontrollably causing a gut-wrenching feeling in the pit of my stomach. I felt sick and my heart felt like it was about to jump out of my chest. Maybe he was dying of an illness or having a secret love affair, but whatever was written inside this envelope could only be upsetting news, dark news. It was heartbreaking seeing him cry like that so I reached over to gently touch his tanned shoulder and whispered, 'It will be alright, honey! Whatever it is, we will get through it!' He continued to sob, now more loudly than ever. I desperately wanted to hug him, but I was too anxious to discover what this dreaded white envelope contained. My hands were shaking. After fumbling and trembling as I took out the folded paper inside, I slowly read the four long pages of neatly written script. Julian was a primary school art teacher who always did have the most beautiful, flowing handwriting and this was no different. His artistic nature was revealed in everything that he created; his paintings, his sketches and his cake decorating.

    I carefully and painstakingly read the first two lengthy paragraphs, which expressed his love for the kids and myself. He also wrote something about being sorry for his distance lately and that he had been very depressed and forever pondering over how he was going to speak to me about this. I kept reading, line after line, as my head started to hurt and a lump formed in my throat, freezing as my eyes were fixated on the same three words, 'I am gay.' 'I am gay.' 'I am gay.' No, it could not be possible. Not at all possible! I must have read it wrong. It seemed like an eternity before I could read every single page, word by word, syllable by syllable, trying anxiously to decide whether this was an insensitive joke, a cryptic message or my worst nightmare. Everything seemed to be in slow motion. I had this mysterious letter in my hands, with Julian crying next to me, and it was as though time had stopped. My mind continued to race like a rewound video, with thoughts of all those years. I recalled the wedding, the birth of our children and the future we had planned. A movie in fast motion, ending before it should. How could my husband of twenty-one years be gay? We had three children, who were now aged sixteen, eighteen and twenty. The questions rapidly flooded my mind,

CHAPTER 1

like an overflowing bathtub. I could not stop the interrogation.

Is this true?
How long have you known?
Are you sure?
Did you ever love me?
Have you been unfaithful?
What does this all mean?

The calmness in my body and my voice as I spoke surprised me, although all I really wanted to do was shout, scream, push him away and rip the letter into tiny little pieces. A voice deep inside told me to keep composed or I may never know what this all really meant. If I argued with Julian, he would only withdraw or run off like he had in the past. He blew his nose into his tartan hanky as he sobbed, 'I never ever wanted to hurt you Leanne. I just had to tell you because I was afraid of what I might do, and you deserve someone so much better than me!'

I had heard something like this before. My father...
He never wanted to 'hurt' his daughters, but he did! Many times. In that old, damp house full of mildewed walls and the smell of disinfectant. Behind the pigeon cages where the coos of pigeons

blocked out the noise. I wanted to trust men, but they continued to let me down. I swore with my whole heart never to let anyone in, never to fully trust a man again. My father was mentally and sexually abusive. A monster. I had once again let my guard down and allowed a man into my life. But Julian was supposed to be different. I thought I could trust him.

Julian and I stayed up the whole night talking, crying and holding each other tighter than we ever had before. I could not remember the last time we had embraced so lovingly. Fortunately, we were on school holidays, since there was no sleep for either of us that hot, January night. My initial thought was that Julian wanted to end the marriage and I was in no way prepared for any of this. But in his four-page, well-written letter, he wrote, 'I hope we can continue our marriage journey, albeit a different one.' Whatever that meant, I was not sure yet. He also expressed his undying love and care for me, stating that the decision would be up to me whether we stayed together or not. A tsunami of emotions fell upon me all at once. Shock, surprise, confusion, betrayal and pain. So much pain. Endless pain that no amount of paracetamol could heal. I needed time to comprehend what this all meant, time to read the letter over and over. I needed answers, to examine the last twenty something years in detail and determine what was real, what was a façade and who this stranger really was lying next to me in my bed. We talked for a very long time, agreeing to work emphatically to strengthen our marriage, to encompass new ways of nurturing our relationship and to be more loving and understanding towards each other. After all, in the past eight years we had not made love, we barely even kissed and had a mild resentment for each other. Julian never outwardly showed me any love or affection unless it was on my birthday or Christmas. He showed his love by helping with cooking dinner, cleaning and being financially supportive.

I could have left him dozens of times over those twenty-two years but each time I came close to walking out the door I stopped myself, thinking my marriage could be a lot worse; he did not drink, gamble or have secret affairs. Marriage was for better or for worse. For many years, I believed that the reason Julian did not want sex and could not get aroused was because he had a medical condition or asexuality. Excuses. I had absolutely no idea that for the last five or six years, he was getting up extra early, not just to exercise on the treadmill in the shed, but to look at gay pornography on the internet. I was not a morning person so he could easily get up at 4.30am, retreat to the lounge room and I would be none the wiser as I slept for another few hours. I wonder how different things would have been if I had walked in on him one morning had I needed to go to the bathroom. It was eventually his guilt and desperate yearning for a male partner that finally led him to telling me of this regular occurrence and much more.

In the next few weeks, Julian and I went through what felt like a 'honeymoon period'. It truly felt like we were discovering each other all over again. I even felt more positive at this stage. Julian was infinitely more affectionate, hugging me at every opportunity and touching me whenever he walked past. He was a new man, more aware of my needs and expressed his love through words and gestures. We decided to write a list of all the things we loved and admired about each other and our expectations within the marriage. Maybe then we could ensure that our relationship would thrive, and our family would stay together. We agreed to go out more as a couple, visiting places we often put aside because of work or the kids. It was incredibly exciting, almost like dating again, and I truly was confident that our love would just get stronger and stronger. I believed wholeheartedly that it would work out for the better. How could it not succeed? Our love was still deep for each other and our family was so important to both of us. Family was everything. If Julian only needed to look at some images of men every

CHAPTER 1

once in a while, I could deal with it and I reminded myself that it could be worse. We walked along the sand on the beach on weekends, eating ice cream and holding hands. I was falling in love all over again with my husband and during this period, I was very happy. I was more attentive to how I dressed, how I did my hair and even watched my weight. I was desperately trying to win my husband's love and devotion and was willing to do whatever it took. I had nothing to lose and everything to gain.

CHAPTER 2

During the night, we found various ways to satisfy each other's needs. We looked at pictures of virile naked guys from the Internet. We ordered some X-rated calendars. I would rub Julian's penis while he caressed my breasts and sucked on my nipples. It felt amazing and we were both incredibly happy and satisfied. For weeks, we deliberately went to bed extra early so we could spend time together, excitedly choosing a picture or video to look at for our arousal. This was a special time until one night, when Julian and I were touching each other. We were looking at a picture of a naked guy in a calendar when Julian uttered, 'He is so hot, yum.' This was too personal for me and I felt as though my heart was ripped out. I suddenly realised that this relationship was not between the two of us. It was always going to be about another guy, whether it was a picture, a video or someone in Julian's mind that he thought of when he was kissing or touching me. This image was supposed to be for our mutual benefit, a tool, a device to help us get aroused. I could not do this anymore. I felt trapped like a fly in a web full of spiders. I was encouraging him to think even more about sex with men, without even realising it. I feared who I had become, and it made me feel exploited and insecure.

> *That feeling of being powerless, a pawn in a game where men are the only winners. The bribes. Money for a look. Dirty. He was supposed to be my father, protecting me but I needed protection from him. His hands were big, rough as sandpaper. I needed to run.*

I started to wonder whether Julian already had sex with men and whether he was now visiting dating websites. Was this whole thing going to blow up in my face like a grenade? I was trying considerably hard to keep my husband content, but I was never going to be a substitute for a hot-blooded man. I did not resemble a man or walk or talk like one. I came to the realisation that if I did not look after myself, I could be a very lonely woman one day. It was imperative that I develop some personal interests away from work and the family. I could catch up more with friends and take up yoga classes again. I was even more determined to look after my physical and mental health. If I did not love and nurture myself, who would?

If I watched television and there were young, attractive gay men on a show or commercial, it made me feel depressed. It triggered a series of emotions and I would suddenly become angry with the actors, even though it had nothing to do with them. I was becoming paranoid, seeing any half decent man as a threat, as someone that Julian might be interested in. This even affected family outings to the football, where I found myself watching his eye contact so much that I just did not enjoy going out anymore. Every minute and every second of every day, I was afraid that he would have an affair. It was my mission, my only focus. I lost all my trust in him since he had been lying to me for all those years. What could I possibly do to keep him faithful, especially now that he had nothing more to lose?

As the weeks passed, I was finding it increasingly challenging to act 'normal' in front of the kids. When they came home from school or work, I made sure that I wiped away my tears and put on my best smile, trying to act like everything was the same as usual. Until one day, when I was not coping with even the smallest tasks. I sat outside on my favourite bench in the garden to pray and I was talking out loud to my deceased mother. I missed her so much and knew that if she were still alive, she would know exactly what to say to make me feel better. I felt so alone. As I sat there in a daze, Sarah, my nineteen-year-old daughter, arrived home from work. She called my name repeatedly as she looked for me, only to discover me hunched over the bench, bawling my eyes out. I tried to reassure Sarah that I just missed Nana and was having a bad day. She always could see right through me like a pane of glass and she knew there was something more that I wasn't revealing. She questioned me over and over until she realised that my distress had something to do with her father. I really did not want to tell her, but I could not lie to her any longer.

When she asked, 'Are you two separating?' I replied, 'Maybe.' She asked if he had been having an affair or something.

'Well, not really,' I said.

After a few more questions, she asked, 'Is Dad gay Mum?'

I was relieved by her question and replied, 'Yes, I'm sorry darling but he is gay.' Sarah asked many of the same questions I did. She looked more shocked than upset at this stage. She told me that he should never have lied to me in the first place. Her first instinct was to protect me, but I knew she loved her Dad too, and it would be hard to know how to react in front of him. Upon discussing this conversation with Julian, we decided to tell the others together as a family.

As we sat together as a family at the dining table, I observed the kids' faces one by one. Brandon looked as though he was going to cry at any moment and Charlotte stared impatiently at us, waiting for our response. I turned to look at Sarah; she put her hand on my shoulder and then buried her head in her hands. Julian quickly looked at me before attempting to explain the situation.

He started by saying, 'I want you to know that I love you,' and the rest was just a blur as he cried hysterically, red-faced and totally distressed.

He eventually managed to tell them the whole story and the reactions of the kids varied greatly. Brandon cried quietly, while observing both Julian and me. The poor kid looked like his whole world was collapsing. Sarah tried to remain calm by asking questions, as much for her siblings' sake than her own. Julian explained that at this stage we were staying together, but we did not know how it was all going to be in the future. We both told them repeatedly that nothing would change our love for them.

The secret was out, at least to the children and me,

and now I just walked on fragile eggshells, waiting for the day that he would take the next step to act on his urges, as he called them. It was frustrating, desperately struggling to hold on to the marriage, holding onto whatever traces we had left. I never was the type of person to give up on what I believed in and I would do whatever I could to make this work, if I managed to stay sane in the process. At times, I wondered whether Julian was trying to make the marriage work as much as me, or was I possibly putting in all the effort for the both of us?

This is about the same time that my regular nightmares began, with the sleepless nights adding to the strain that I lived with daily. The dreams followed a familiar theme. Julian would go missing for hours and then I would find him. In the dream, he would act coldly towards me, saying that he was only talking to a guy from work and that I should stop being so paranoid. They were only dreams, I know, but they felt so damned real that I repeatedly awoke in a sweat, gasping for breath. There were other nights where I simply could not get to sleep at all, lying in bed for hours and hours, feeling like I was living someone else's life, praying that one day, everything would be magically back to normal.

When I was young, I slept in the middle of my parents until I was about five years old. There were

CHAPTER 2

so many restless nights. I needed sleep but I woke constantly. I was a frightened little lamb, longing for security and to be rescued from the abuse. That kind of fear never leaves you; it just overshadows every other part of your life. Why couldn't I just erase that part of my life like you would erase pencil when you didn't like what you had written?

My insecurities were eating me alive and I still had so many questions that I needed answers to. For weeks, I kept asking the same things, driving him mad, trying to put all the pieces of the puzzle together. I asked Julian if he ever thought of me when we kissed and he hesitated before replying, 'Sometimes.' Wrong bloody answer! I could not change who he was or who he thought about; I just desperately needed to know that he cared for me. I still loved him, and I did not want to be some substandard substitute for a man, a stand-in until the real thing came along. Like one of those American soap operas, I was holding on to a romantic notion that one day Julian would tell me that he truly loved me, only me, and that when we kissed, he thought of me, just me. I wasn't sure how long I could keep thinking like this, growing more distrustful as time went on. I made an appointment to see my counsellor because my mental and physical health were suffering considerably. My children said I was getting too thin and others said I looked tired and drained. I just lived each day as it came, but I was not happy.

I never sought after another man during the marriage simply because my sexual needs were not being fulfilled. There were many ways to satisfy myself, without being unfaithful. I wanted my husband to be my 'ideal man' and marriage was supposed to be for life, as far as I was concerned. I assumed that we would grow old together, have lots of cute grandchildren and then make travel plans for our retirement. I spoke to my counsellor and she could not give me the answers I wanted to hear. She listened sympathetically, as usual, and gave me some useful advice, but she obviously did not have a crystal ball to predict the future. I would have gone and bought her a crystal ball, if I knew it would have really helped. I asked her whether it was possible for a mixed orientation couple to live happily ever after and she basically told me that it was not 'impossible' and only time would tell. I prayed for hope, peace and happiness.

The meltdowns started in the next few weeks. They always started in the same way. I had so many questions, tough questions that never produced the responses that I yearned for. Julian's silence killed me considerably more than any learned response that I had heard before. Knowing now that he thought of men throughout the whole marriage was too hard to accept. I felt like a wounded animal, like a knife was being pushed deeper and deeper into my heart. My trust in him had vanished, causing Julian to be resentful of the fact that I had lost faith in him.

Arguments were common in the house when I was growing up. Mum and Dad would fight during the night. I never knew what the arguments were over. Was it my fault? Could I have stopped them? Apparently, Dad threatened to kill himself over and over. Why did he go to jail? I heard years later that he did. Was it really because he did not pay his taxes? I wished that he stayed there longer so we could all have some peace.

I cried morning, afternoon and night. Like Alice in Wonderland, the pool of tears would amount to an ocean had I collected them. Unremittingly, I struggled to process this fearful nightmare that was now my life. When I was at my lowest ebb, all I wanted was to feel his warm embrace, but this was never going to happen. Alternatively, my children were extremely loving, hugging me more often than usual and always checking in during the day. When I wasn't sobbing, I did the best I could to ensure that they were coping as well, but I was not there for them much at that time since I could not even help myself. Ironically, in the past if I was upset because of an argument with a friend or a work colleague, Julian would be the one I would lean on, and now he was the one who was causing all this misery. I was living in trepidation that he would act on his feelings for men and he could not give me a definite promise that he would not. I cried uncontrollably on a regular basis for months. Sometimes Julian cried too, telling me multiple times that he really wanted the marriage to work. I believed him. We stayed up for hours on many occasions. Often, I would ask a question that led onto other questions, trying to seek some reassurance that I would ultimately never receive. My heart was slowly breaking into pieces and everything I knew was crumbling before my eyes like a house of cards. All I could do was pray to God that he would help me through this pain, one slow day after another. If the pain were from a physical encounter, I would be at the hospital having treatment, but the pain was emotional, invisible to the eye. Silent suffering. The kids went about their normal routine, but we were all in shock, zombies in a house that once felt like a home.

On several occasions, I spoke to my counsellor about my insecurities and fear for the future. How were the kids and I going to cope? I told her that I felt like I was losing my mind at times, incessantly checking Julian's laptop history, jumping at every possible chance to investigate the websites he had been on that day, that week. I seized every opportunity, whether that was when he had a shower, went to the shops or had a nap. I was controlled by the laptop, much like a gambler and Pokies. Of course, most times it was the same, his history revealed that he was looking at videos and pictures of hot guys having sex in every possible position. I would have a quick look, only to feel revolted, wounded and unloved. It became an obsession. I needed to check the laptop, hoping that one day I would inspect the laptop history and there would be no evidence of his disloyalty. When this occurred, it would just entice me to check even more. I was wasting so much time and energy confirming what I already suspected. I knew that he was never going to stop, but I prayed that he would.

My father had a filthy cardboard box in the shed, filled with horrible magazines of naked women. One day I saw him looking at them. We all knew about his dirty little secret. If only he just looked at magazines and left others alone. My two eldest sisters married young so that they could leave the house and not have to face him every day. I wanted to leave with them, but I was stuck. One day, I too would experience freedom, but the fear does not leave you. Running away does not help.

I just could not comprehend how he could 'love' me but still felt compelled to look at gay pornography. The Internet was the 'other woman,' although in this case it was the 'other man.' I was competing with these websites and it looked as though I would never be the victor. In an outburst of rage, I questioned Julian about all the cards from Valentine's days, birthdays and wedding anniversaries. They were swarming with words of love and devotion, and forever after. I asked him if the written words and sentiments were blatant lies, the truth or just a cover up. He sat there in silence, ruminating over this simple question, not wanting to say the wrong answer. Instead of telling me what I wanted to hear, he resolved to tell me the truth, whether it hurt or not, for fear of perpetuating the deception of the past twenty-one years.

He paused then uttered, 'I was just keeping up the act. I really believed with time we could make this work.'

My heart sank and I asked him through tears if he ever loved me.

He responded by saying, 'I did…do love you in my own, unique way.'

He uttered that it had taken him too long to be ready to tell the family and me about his sexuality.

'At the time of writing the cards I had to continue to act as if everything was fine.'

This meant that he had to write cards as a husband would. My heartbeat was racing a million miles an hour as I felt exploited, dejected and demoralised. As my infuriation increased, I proceeded to ask if the paintings he painted of us all as a happy family meant anything to him. On the bottom of the painting he wrote, 'My loving family, I hope our family grows stronger and stronger.' What did this all mean? In a puerile manner, he aggressively ripped the paintings from the wall, breaking them and throwing them piece by piece in the rubbish bin.

Violence, yelling and voices screaming. I was just a small child, surrounded by angry adults. I wished that I could be anywhere but in that house. My whole body shook. We can't tell anyone, not our Aunty or Uncle, especially not the neighbours. We must live silently with the violence. It's our family secret. Just crawl into a ball and act as if nothing happened.

CHAPTER 3

It grieved me that we could not even discuss things civilly anymore, but I did not attempt to restore the wretched paintings. The pictures were a mirror of our marriage, broken and irreparable. I had reached the point of not being able to even look at his face at times. He was now a stranger to me and my husband as I had known him did not exist anymore. He died. There was no turning back. The words on the last Valentine's Day card stood out before my eyes. He wrote, 'Whatever happens I will always love you.' It gave me the impression that Julian could foresee our separation, but I was not sure who he thought would leave the marriage. I told him that I did not want a card from him ever again since I could never again believe a single word he wrote.

I booked in to see my counsellor the next day and asked her, as I had before, if she believed that our relationship had any chance of surviving, although it would never be the same. She tried to set my mind at rest by asserting that Julian had not been unfaithful thus far and he was generally an honest person. She also reminded me of the fact that the two of us were both working together on the same goal, to improve our marriage and renegotiate the rules of our new situation. As much as I liked to have everything under control, there really was nothing else I could do, other than to play the waiting game and see how it all worked out. Even heterosexual couples have no guarantee that their marriage will last, and it is not uncommon for married people to glance at someone they find attractive. I tried to convince myself that if I had faith and love, nothing would go wrong. I attempted to enjoy my time with Julian, focusing on the present and not worrying about the future. I made it my goal to be more positive, to not overreact to everything. It was obvious that our relationship and our family would need time for us all to adjust, so I just needed to be patient. Simple.

Some days were amazing, and I felt optimistic and confident that life would get better, and it was not going to be the end of the world after all. Nevertheless, there were days and weeks that followed where I felt so despondent that I somehow invited an argument, only resulting in more bitterness and tears. I wanted answers to so many questions, constantly interrogating Julian, but often not getting the answers that I hoped for or no answer at all. His silence and long pauses only increased my paranoia. This was exacerbated by the fact that he was looking at gay pornography websites every second day and withholding information from me. Further probing disclosed more and more secrets and lies. I queried Julian as to why he could not get money out from the bank to pay for petrol. He told me that funds were taken without his approval, and that he placed a hold on his credit card and ordered another, which seemed to be taking forever to arrive. It was not until several weeks later that he told me that the money was being debited for a gay animation site, but I believed that it was something more. He was always lecturing the children about not giving personal details like bank accounts over the Internet if the site was not secure. What a hypocrite. He had signed up to a dating site as well, apparently just to look but not to ever meet up with anyone. I could see all the messages in the trash folder. Julian said he never intended to meet up, but as far as I was concerned, he had overstepped the mark, and this was as good as an affair. I felt so sick that I vomited in the bathroom, releasing not only my lunch but also the stress and burdens I had been holding inside for way too long.

I could never deal with waste. Money wasted. Bills not paid. Mummy was in tears as they repossessed our fridge and television. We could not afford them anymore. She told us not to worry, we would be fine. We would cope. Mum tried her utmost to protect and provide for us. That's what parents do, and I must do the same now.

I went to my bedroom, sat at the desk and divided a piece of paper in two halves. I wrote down all the reasons that we should or should not stay together.

Stay together for the kids
We will be better off financially if he stays
We still care for each other
It is too painful to stay married when I know his secret
It gives us a chance to move forward on our own
The constant fighting must stop, we are both going crazy

I also recorded all my fears and insecurities regarding our potential split. I wondered whether I would cope financially and having to manage everything on my own. Writing was cleansing for me, releasing my worries and handing them over to paper. My main trepidation now was how I would cope financially, but with some careful planning I realised that I would manage. I could take on some tutoring to earn some extra cash on the side and tighten up some of my expenses. My other concern was loneliness, yet I had many friends and a wonderful family. I thought about the hobbies that I never got around to, such as dancing, swimming and writing. If I was honest with myself, I had a deep-seated fear of the unknown and going against my traditional values that marriage was forever. I had decisions to make and it was never going to be easy, whichever way I decided. The truth is, my marriage was a sham, a fraud and my adult children would be better off if the marriage ended because it was a toxic relationship. The venom was spreading daily to all of us. What type of message was I giving the children if I stayed? I had tried so hard to salvage what was left, but I had nothing left to give. I felt empty and utterly exhausted. Julian outwardly refused counselling, so it was evident that we just had to go our separate ways. It takes two to tango and two to make a marriage work. That feeling of entrapment was a constant reminder of my childhood.

The tiredness, fear, bed-wetting. Trapped in a house with a monster, but no escape.

My bed wetting days were long gone, and Julian was far from a monster, but living a lie was a beast like no other. The next day I went to work as normal, turning up a little late through pure exhaustion. My work mates, Jill and Mary knew something was wrong straightaway, as soon as they saw my expression.

'Are you OK?' Mary enquired.

I just burst into tears, unable to contain my feelings any longer, disclosing the secret that I had been keeping for months. I never could hide anything from these two friends who knew me like the back of their hands. To this day, I am grateful for all their support on my journey to recovery. We went across the road for coffee, where I blurted out everything that happened from the very beginning until now. Jill was so shocked, asking if he was sure that he was gay and whether he was just confused. Mary was angry at Julian for waiting so long to tell me and destroying my life and the children's lives. She had gay family members, but none of them had done such a thing as marry a woman. They just stayed single. I cried and cried, realising that holding all my feelings in was not productive for anyone and it was time to start telling my family and friends the truth. My loyal friends' comforting advice and hugs during the next few months kept me going, as tough as it was.

Life at home, after finally making the decision to separate, created additional problems in our day to day living arrangements. We set down the ground rules, agreeing that we would continue to sleep in the same bed, but just giving each other a brief hug before sleeping. We did not kiss anymore, not even on the cheek. We also agreed that we would not date other people until the separation because this would only make things too complicated for us and the children. I told Julian that I could not prevent him from looking at gay pornography, but I felt that he was viewing these sites too much. Telling him to limit the pornography was like suggesting that an alcoholic only consume alcohol twice a week. I secretly decided on a plan of action for my and the kids' future, a kind of survival kit. I felt positive for a few days, but this was not to last as the tears and sadness were all-encompassing. I took a few days off work to breathe and reassess my life, my goals, my survival strategies. My focus shifted from Julian to my needs. I deserved kindness in my life, I craved romance, communication and consideration. I had missed out on so much in the last twenty odd years. I was sick and tired of being a substitute for someone else's true desires. Surely, I deserved more. The children and I had suffered, and it was time to prioritise our emotional health. I encouraged the kids to speak to a counsellor and tell their closest friends about the separation if they felt comfortable and thought that it would help. My son, Brandon, spoke to a counsellor that he had seen several times in the past for anxiety and she helped him to realise that his Dad was still the same father he had always known. The counselling helped Brandon realise the fact that Julian was gay was totally separate to their father-son relationship. The girls were not ready to seek any form of counselling, preferring to talk to their closest friends. Brandon, on the other hand, could not tell his friends, saying he just did not know how to talk about it. I tried to catch up with friends as well, no longer making excuses. I stood up for myself more and slowly regained that person I used to be.

> *When I moved out of my parents' house, I felt more in control than I ever had. I was not going to be pressured into anything ever again. I knew I had to do whatever it took to protect myself and my health. I moved to the west side of the city to start a new life, finish my studies and gain my confidence.*

Gradually, I came to terms with the fact that Julian was gay. I wasn't jumping for joy over it, but I had accepted it. There was no point denying it or sweeping it under the carpet. Julian said he may never even act on his urges, but this was little consolation for the feelings of rejection, betrayal and a constant feeling that a black cloud was hanging over my head. I always wished to be that special lady in someone's life, not just a wife and mother, a woman who was cherished, loved wholeheartedly and admired. For many years, I tried relentlessly to please my husband, but never felt that he did the same, at least not in ways that I wanted him to. Julian never initiated sex and often it was over before it started, or it just never happened. When we made the decision to physically separate at the end of the year, we agreed that the separation could be a trial, but deep down we both knew that our marriage would never be the same again.

Our long-time friend, Rob, was trying to support both of us, attempting to save our doomed marriage. He was always controversial in the way he handled people and situations, so Julian refused to tell Rob because of Rob's extreme views on gay people. One afternoon I rang Rob, in tears, telling him to come over because I was so drained and jaded with keeping up appearances and pretending. I couldn't do it anymore. I slowly broke the news to Rob, our friend of over twenty years, explaining the revelation and how it all came about. It would be an understatement to say he was shocked, as he sat with his mouth wide open and a perplexed look on his face. His questions kept coming, but he did not want to believe the truth.

Julian's long-time mate, Rob, thought that if he took Julian for a drive, he could instil fear into him to realise how wrong he was and that his marriage was worth fighting for. Rob bluntly told Julian that he had an addiction to pornography, not dissimilar to a drug addiction. He also told him that the pornography sites were completely unrealistic, nothing like real life and that men generally don't participate in group sex, don't have oversized penises and long-lasting erections. He said he would never really know if he was homosexual or bisexual if he was continually viewing these corrupt videos. He also said if he continued like this, he would end up dead in a gutter with a sexually transmitted infection.

Rob's views and speech shocked and infuriated Julian. He did avoid watching pornography for an entire week, but he became agitated, aggressive and rude in the process. It was like he was genuinely having withdrawal symptoms and would need a 'fix.' As much as I prayed that he would not view these sites, I knew it was inevitable. His mood only worsened. I went out with friends more than usual to get a break from the uncomfortable feeling of being at home. There was no peace, not at home or even when I slept.

CHAPTER 4

I decided to go to Centrelink the following week to apply for financial assistance for the girls while they were at university and on a low income. We were now separated but living under the same roof and were beginning to plan for Julian to move out at the end of the year. I slowly progressed in the queue, struggling to hold back tears, but when I finally spoke to the Customer Service Assistant, I broke down into a complete mess. She handed me a tissue and I found it almost impossible to utter a word. My eyes were blinded from tears, my nose red and sore, like that feeling when you have a bad cold. This lady was so understanding, placing me ahead of many others in the queue and taking me directly to the social worker. The social worker asked a lot of questions regarding a chance of reconciliation and I just told him that there was absolutely no way we could stay together. I drooped forward on the black swivel chair, like a person in a trance, nodding my head and signing forms that made no sense to me at all.

When I got home, I felt gutted. I rang my older sister, Maree, who was the only person in my family that I had told at that stage. She lived interstate and I trusted her implicitly, knowing she could keep a secret if her life depended on it. She had also been through a divorce many years earlier, so she knew all the right things to say to give me some comfort. She listened patiently as I told her that Julian and I could not stay together and how my whole world was falling apart. Maree and her second husband got along well with Julian, but she was there for me right now and understood wholeheartedly. The pain of separation was just so insufferable, with reminders of the marriage everywhere I looked. The photographs, the jewellery, letters addressed in both names. Memories.

Apart from the ultimate separation, we decided that by the end of the year we would finish the house renovations, sort our finances and discuss the legalities of our assets. There was also the issue of whether the kids wanted to stay in the family home and live with me or move with their Dad. The decision would be theirs to make. I really did not want any of them to move, but if they decided to live with Julian, the only thing that mattered was their happiness. By the end of the year, our youngest, Charlotte would be finished with her VCE. As we discussed our future and the kids, the sadness in Julian's eyes mirrored the grief in my heart. Twenty something years to be untangled, like an endless ball of string. A family unit to be separated from five to four people. My life was in limbo whilst living together and I struggled to come to terms with the changes. It killed me inside to see how it was affecting the kids, sad faces, that uncertain look that nothing would ever be the same. But I knew it was time to seek further help and support from people who knew exactly how I was feeling.

I searched the Internet for advice and support and found boundless information that I needed to filter through. Some straight partners had suffered horrific abuse, others decided to stay together and have an open marriage. I finally found an email address of the administrator of a support network for straight spouses whose partners had revealed that they were either gay, lesbian or transgender. Her name was Wendy and she was incredibly caring, informative and an amazing listener. She recommended that I join the Facebook support group, which had members from all over Australia and some from the US. I was surprised that there were literally hundreds of people in this group alone, not counting the numbers in other groups or those who are still in the closet. This group was based in my State and every single member had been married to, or in a relationship with a partner who came out as either gay, bisexual or transsexual. Some were separated or divorced, and a minority chose to stay together. She mentioned that the Melbourne group met up for coffee occasionally if I was interested in going along. I had never opened a Facebook account previously, mainly because I worked in a school and I wanted to keep my private life and work life separate. I decided to start an account under a pseudonym, without a profile picture to remain anonymous. After talking to Wendy, I realised that I was far from alone. I was astounded and could not believe how many people in Australia had experienced the exact type of relationship break-up that I had. Their story was my story. I was determined to not let this be the end of my life as I was only fifty years old after all. If I surrounded myself with supportive people, perhaps in time I would heal and live a happy, fulfilling life. I joined the support group and it proved to be an immense step towards my recovery. I learnt how to cope with life a lot better after reading member's posts and posting my own thoughts and feelings. Everyone was incredibly compassionate, welcoming and understanding. Each member was full of amazing advice. It was as though God had found the sweetest, kindest people on Earth and placed them all in this group. As I started to get my head above water, I suddenly realised that my kids were not coping. I was oblivious to their troubled minds while I was immersed in my own sorrow. My son Brandon, who is very sensitive, was anxious, even more than usual. His counselling sessions needed to be increased to help him deal with all the changes in our family. My youngest daughter, Charlotte was trying desperately to focus on her studies, but it all got too much. She finally admitted that it was overwhelming and stressful, and she was losing her concentration. This would have taken an immense amount of courage for Charlotte as she was always the strong, proud one and did not like to show her feelings, always focusing on how others were feeling.

Charlotte and Brandon fought with each other constantly over the following two weeks, mostly over trivial things. I was just not managing at times either. Their constant bickering created more tension in the house. I spoke to them both separately, listening sorrowfully as they told me of their worries. I could not hold back the tears, weeping as they both told me that they felt distressed and could not cope with their daily lives anymore. I let them know that I understood how hard this was for them both and that I loved them very much, hoping they would understand the other's point of view. The tension died down after a few days and Charlotte and Brandon were more focused on what they had to do, whether that was work or study. In many ways, it brought them closer together as they realised that they were both feeling the same way.

Five months after the revelation, I thought about what I wanted out of life, attempting to connect with who I was before I met Julian. I grappled with my thoughts, realising that I had changed dramatically in the last twenty years. I really needed to know who I was now, as a woman in her fifties, not as a mother or as a wife or employee. I reflected on why I was initially attracted to Julian and how I did not pick up on any signs that he was gay. Why was I blind to the obvious? I assumed that he was simply a gentle soul and that he was quite refreshing in my life, where other men had been abusive or arrogant.

In retrospect, my whole life before marriage had been about escaping from anyone or anything that made me feel anxious or uneasy. I had not once stopped to think about what really happened to me all those years ago as a child in the backyard when no one could hear me. I had blocked it out completely. Now, I could feel the tears of terror surfacing, even when I tried to remember it all for just a few seconds. Remembering was just too painful, but I knew that those horrific experiences influenced my life choices. For many of my adult years, I was just searching for somewhere, anywhere that I could feel safe. Did I subconsciously choose Julian because I knew he was never going to be physically or sexually abusive? If I knew all those years ago that I would still be hurt by Julian in other ways, then I would not have married him. Retrospect is gold.

    Julian was moody and distant at times but not aggressive or controlling in any way. I would not have stayed married for twenty-one years had he been. His calmness and nurturing manner made me feel safe. He was never physically or sexually abusive, but he did not show affection in the ways that I craved so desperately. I could never seek love elsewhere because it was my fervent belief that marriage was for life, for better or worse. The marriage could have been a lot worse. Of course, he was grouchy at times, distant and a little hurtful, but not always intentionally. I could be moody too, especially when I was hormonal and due for my period. His apparent lack of empathy and affection at times could possibly have been due to a touch of Asperger's. This also explained his consistent routine of work, home, dinner, coffee, falling asleep watching television and then off to bed by 9.30pm. There was no deviation from this pattern unless we occasionally had visitors and even then, he struggled to stay awake. I remember one time when our friend Rob came over unexpectedly. Julian sat quietly on the couch in the other room and fell asleep. He never wanted to go out much or travel. I really longed for some couple time together, but it was just not worth the effort. I could lead the horse to water, but it was ultimately up to the horse to drink the water. We had become strangers living under the same roof and a day never passed where I did not mourn the love that we once shared.

I had numerous recurring dreams during the marriage. Always the same, night after night. In the dream, I was not married but just dating and my boyfriend had disappeared, and I could not find him. I did not even know who I was dating. It reflected my subconscious, the feeling that I was on my own and I could not find a way to Julian's heart. I craved love, deep love that a couple should have for each other. Normal love. I wore a wedding ring on my left hand but what did it really symbolise? I felt lonely, unloved and rejected. Passion was non-existent in my life and nothing I could do was going to change that. There was no intimacy, no sex for almost ten years. There were times when I was too tired anyway, but sometimes I felt aroused and had to erase the thoughts from my mind, resigning myself to reading instead. I read a lot of novels over those years.

Arguments would transpire now and then when I suggested that he see a doctor about his enduring lack of ability to have sex and hold an erection. We would occasionally kiss after watching a movie, but Julian could almost never get an erection and when he did it would only last about 10 seconds. Obviously, this was not long enough for us to have sex and this would routinely lead him to saying, 'There is no point continuing. Let's just go to sleep.' He argued that it was either a medical condition or that he simply did not need sex like most other men. Excuses. Lots of excuses. Repeatedly I felt deflated, unloved, unworthy and unattractive, ultimately agreeing with Julian that there was no point continuing and being affectionate as it only caused more pain. He would not see a doctor because he apparently did not want the side effects from any medications for erectile dysfunction. At the time, I felt sorry for him, believing he would rectify the problem if he could and it was not the end of the world if I never had sex again.

I did not consider this at the time, but if he did just have problems with getting an erection then why didn't he at least just touch or hug me? I justified this by believing that Julian was on the Autism spectrum, causing his lack of affection, even trepidation of touch. I tried a range of techniques to attract Julian, including buying the most expensive, sexiest lingerie I could purchase. I felt excited that we would be in for a passionate night, only to be told that he was just too tired, rolling over to sleep. I cried myself to sleep. After numerous attempts, I decided I had to dream of what it would be like to have passionate sex again, often fantasising about men from work. If only I knew then that Julian was going to sleep early to avoid contact with me and to ensure he could get up early to watch his favourite porn sites. I would have left him in a heartbeat if I knew all this. My moral compass told me that spending a lot of time viewing other men was as good as cheating! It still makes me livid, just thinking about the fact that I was being lied to all that time and I had to wait until I was in my 50s before I knew the truth and have a chance to move on with my life, to live an authentic life.

Many other people probably would have left him anyway, but I still loved him, and I believed that marriage was forever. I was not perfect either, I had anxiety and sometimes overreacted to situations. Julian did have some wonderful caring qualities, showing his love by helping around the house, especially when I was ill or felt a bit down. He could also be painfully frustrating, never feeling the need to carry his phone with him to contact the children or myself and he often did not stand up for us when we conflicted with others because he was afraid of losing face.

CHAPTER 5

The following months of living together would prove to be one of the hardest and most intense times of my life, not discounting my horrendous childhood and the distress of having to live with my abusive father. That uncomfortable and painful feeling, like your heart is being ripped out, the powerless, breathlessness and the constant fear, were all too familiar. Julian was supposed to be the one who saved me from those fears, but now he was causing me just as much pain as my despicable father. I always valued Julian's honesty and openness. If there was one person that I believed would tell me the truth no matter what it would have been him. He could not even tell a white lie when he needed a day off work, eternally genuine.

It brought me back again to the pain of living with a father who was abusive, verbally and sexually. My mum couldn't save me then and no one else could now, only myself. I remember hiding behind my mother, especially in social situations. I was generally scared of any male who was not part of the family. In the evenings when we watched television together as a family, I would sit close to mum, leaning in close and making sure that my dreaded father was nowhere next to me. I am sure that she knew what I was doing, protecting and shielding myself from my biggest fear. Distrust of men. I thought that I had built up that trust of the opposite sex, believing that I had nothing to fear. But here I was, my entire body trembling, the tears engulfing me, and I could not breathe through my red, blocked nose. Why could I not trust any man in my life? My father's hands were always a reminder of what he had done in the backyard, when no one could hear my screams. What was the point of screaming? Who would hear? Who would care? He touched all six of his daughters, under the cover of his pigeon cages. I do not dislike pigeons, they were trapped like I was, only let out when it suited him. I was also trapped in a home filled with panic and deep secrets. For years, I wanted to tell someone, anyone, but if I did, they might have thought I was crazy or telling lies. After all, I wet the bed most nights and I never wanted anyone to discover that. People would judge me and where on Earth would I go?

I loved my mum wholeheartedly, was constantly by her side, but I knew she would never leave my Dad. My sisters were silently going through the same thing, although we never confided in each other at the time. It breaks my heart as a parent, thinking back to what we all went through and the consequences it had on all our lives. The effects on my siblings ranged from alcoholism and drug abuse, to mental illness, and the aftermath would continue. In my teens, I wore layers and layers of clothes so that nobody could see my body shape and later became anorexic in my twenties. It became impossible to live in my parents' house, causing me to take an overdose of pills at twenty-one years old. This was the time that I started counselling sessions and divulging everything to my siblings. It would take another five years until I could finally believe in myself and my strengths. I managed to overcome a lot of adversity, moving to the other side of Melbourne to start afresh. A new life. I completed a Bachelor of Education within four years and I have never looked back since. The only regret I have is the quality time I could have spent with Mum while I was studying at a University that was two hours away. But I did spend some time with her after Dad passed away, both in her unit and later the nursing home. Perhaps I should have felt some sort of grief when he died, but I only felt pure relief from the fact that I would never ever have to face him or his dirty, wrinkly hands so long as I lived. I was six months pregnant with my third child, Charlotte when my father died and I remember crying incessantly at the funeral, thinking, thank God, my children would never have to spend time with him. Thank God, we could roam this Earth where he would never be a part of it. I could feel all eyes on me from every direction as I sobbed, trying in vain to stop crying but to no avail.

The constant fear and deep-seated disgust that I felt in my younger years was relived as I regularly checked Julian's laptop. I searched the history tab for viewed websites, feeling insecure and utterly compelled to investigate what he was doing when the kids and I were not home. My fears were always authenticated, as I found more evidence of images of 'hot males,' pornography and images of AFL footballers. I was literally making myself ill, checking the laptop at every opportunity. But I could not stop this incessant desire to know what he was thinking about. Mostly, I was hoping to discover that he was not searching for men on the internet, but I was also a little curious to get inside his thoughts and to try to understand him.

Again, I asked myself, were there any obvious signs that I missed? Could I have prevented this? I could not discern whether I had inadvertently ignored the signs that Julian was gay or whether he had become so proficient at lying that it was not obvious. I know now that it was the latter and it was pointless looking back to analyse every part of the marriage in those twenty-one years. My head was heavy and aching constantly as I tried to process everything. No amount of paracetamol would ease the pain that I felt in my entire body from my head to my aching feet.

I was still massively fearful of the future for many reasons, pondering how I would survive financially and emotionally, now in my fifties with three young adults to support and on one low income. I did not want a life of poverty for the kids and me, so I sat down and planned my future, listing my fears on one side and the solutions on the other side. I kept reminding myself that I could and would get through this. After all, I had survived worse and came out on the other side a stronger person. There were plenty of positives in my life, including my precious kids, wonderful family, beautiful friends and a secure job that I loved. Life would never be boring or lonely, whether I ever had another relationship or not. My marriage did not define me as a person, and I think there lay the solution to overcoming the separation.

It was a huge relief once I felt strong enough to tell others. Thankfully, their response was to provide support and understanding. Counselling helped me to realise that it was not my fault. It sounds obvious, but it is strange how we often internalise things and feel that we somehow contributed to the problem. As I started to feel better, I could see that the kids were also coping better. I needed to pierce the bubble of despair that had enclosed me for many months. It was important for the wellbeing of all of us, that Julian and I remained amicable, at the very least in front of the kids. There were nevertheless times during the remaining months of living together that we quarrelled over the silliest, most trivial things, trying to somehow adjust from being a part of a married couple to two separate people. There were also times when I genuinely felt that Julian was becoming even more distant, even as a friend. I felt invisible in the house, noticing an icy chill as he passed me. He spoke less and less, walking around the house as if he were the only person in it. When I finally got the courage to approach him, he explained that he was acting this way because he did not want to get too close for fear of getting too involved or leading me on. This angered me somewhat, especially when a song would come on, recollecting how deeply I used to love Julian. If Tina Arena or Toni Braxton songs came on the radio, I would be taken back to 1994, smiling and believing that life could not get any better. We were once a team to be reckoned with and we could beat anything, or so it seemed. If I had a dollar for every tear that I cried during this period, I would be one wealthy woman!

I mostly kept my thoughts to myself, not wanting to upset anyone else. I did not want to drag my friends down into my pool of hopelessness. What I did discover was that practising mindfulness exercises helped enormously, taking a few minutes a day to stop what I was doing and concentrate on my breathing. Strangely enough, it was like breathing normally was something I needed to learn all over again. Recovery was not going to happen overnight, but I had to start with the basics. One tiny step at a time.

CHAPTER 6

It was interesting, and even humorous, how various people in my life reacted when I told them the reason for my separation. There were those people who apparently had a gut feeling that something was amiss, like an epiphany. People also reacted in the most comical ways.

> *I did notice he had a slight lisp.*
> *He always was very creative and neat.*
> *He could make lovely cup-cakes.*
> *He wasn't great at sports, was he?*
> *He was so quiet and very gentle with animals.*
> *The moustache should have been a give-away, I guess.*

Others were more astonished, believing that his coming out could be a phase or a misunderstanding.

But he fathered three children.
He married a woman though.
He was faithful for all those years.
He doesn't look gay!

In retrospect, my own reaction could have been similar.

Why doesn't my husband want to have sex?
Why is he not affectionate?
How come sexy lingerie has no effect on him?
Why does he appear embarrassed and uneasy around some men?

My closest friends were equally supportive and angry at the same time, incensed with the fact that he left it such a long time to tell me the truth about his sexual preference, whereas many others admired the way he was being honest and brave. The latter angered me because they could not see the effect this whole thing had taken on the kids and me. Of course, I always have been encouraging of people who are true to their sexuality, but I just don't think many people truly understand the devastation on the partner and children, when men or women 'hide' behind their spouse, forcing them into the closet as well. It hurts profoundly and is exceptionally different to a breakup that occurs because of irreconcilable differences. It is also different to when a partner dies because although it is like a death to a certain degree, the partner is still there, inadvertently reminding you of the lies, deceit and sham of a marriage you once had. What a kick in the arse! Excuse the language.

Some people would tell you that sexuality is pre-determined in the womb, before we are born. If this is true, then we all need to change our preconceived ideas that men and women should remain heterosexual. My mother in law, Maria, would tell me that Julian was such a gentle child who protected animals and was often glued to her hip, not wanting to socialise or interact with others. Even in his early twenties he preferred to stay at home on weekends, watching television or drawing. I later found out that Julian knew in his early teens that he was attracted to the same sex, shunning close contact with other males, fearful that they would realise his feelings. He would have one such 'friend' that he spent a lot of time with when he was about twenty-three years old. They would touch each other and kiss in the house when Maria was not home. This went on for about a year, until the day that his strict Catholic mother walked in on them kissing in the lounge room. Maria was horrified, shouting expletives at the two of them, insisting that his friend never set foot in the house again. She reprimanded Julian and demanded that he set a better example to his younger brother, forcing him to choose between his boyfriend or the family. The choice was obvious, but little did his mother know that he would resent her for the rest of her life. His sister had committed suicide several years earlier and he did not want to cause anymore sorrow to his mother who had single-handedly raised eleven children on her own. He could have rebelled against her, though it was his submissive nature that stopped him from living the life he truly wanted.

The irony is that twenty years on, Julian would have two gay nephews and one gay niece who were openly accepted by Julian's mother. It was hard to tell whether her change in attitude was because of the current times or Maria's age that let her accept their sexuality and their partners so lovingly. Maybe it would be different if they were her own children and the possibility of directed judgement from the community. Maria never told me about what happened with Julian and his friend all those years ago, perhaps believing that he had somehow changed and magically become heterosexual. Of course, marrying the opposite sex makes you heterosexual, doesn't it? Well that is what society once believed anyway. Many believed that if someone appeared to be in a happy marriage, then it protected them from questioning and judgement. Fearing his mother's disappointment, Julian waited until Maria was terminally ill to tell me that he was gay in that four-page letter. She would never be disappointed.

Thinking back, there were many other 'signs' that I was totally oblivious to during our courting and twenty-one-year marriage. Notably, the lack of male friends, avoiding conversations that would make him seem less of a 'bloke' or appearing embarrassed or even awkward at times. By hanging out with women, he would never be faced with uncomfortable topics like sexy women, fishing, golf, building projects or anything else that stereotypical males discussed when women were not around. He would much prefer to discuss cake recipes, artwork or gardening. At least at work he could nurture his interests, teaching Art and organising kitchen garden programs. Work was an escape from his constant inner struggles, a focal point of his life and a place that he could be himself.

As the months ensued after his revelation, my hybrid of emotions on the 'roller coaster ride' progressed from disbelief, anger and betrayal to insecurity, stress and frustration. There would be some tumultuous times ahead that the kids and I never saw coming. It would start with a discussion, mostly one sided, where I would ask Julian a question, attempting to understand how everything got to this stage. One night as we walked, I asked why he did not tell me earlier because I would have been younger and had a higher chance of rebuilding my life. It was just a question. His face reddened as he got angry, shouting that he felt trapped and held back, sparking a violent argument that caused me to scream at him in public. I ran home, faster than I ever had in my life, panting and out of breath. It seemed like hours before I reached the front gate, but I continued around the corner to the local park where I knew my eldest daughter, Sarah, was sitting with her friend Kerry. I tried to speak, but my words were incoherent, and I found I could not even breathe properly. Sarah was anxious about my well-being and I felt like I had an out of body experience. I just continued to cry hysterically, feeling as though Julian had no empathy or conscience and I truly believed that he did not care if I lived or died. It was the lowest ebb of my life and if it were not for my beautiful, extraordinary children, I would never have survived. I was almost ready to just end it all that night.

Sarah rang my sister Rosie and handed me the phone, whereby I could barely utter a reply. Rosie spoke clearly and slowly, saying 'Take some deep breaths in through your nose and out from your mouth.' I listened between each laboured breath and sniffle, shaking uncontrollably, willing myself to listen to my big sister's comforting voice. I wished that my dear mother was still alive to hold me and tell me that everything would be fine, but I had my sister who resembled her so much and I truly believe she saved my life that night. It was not easy to focus on her wise words of advice, so she promised that she would write a text of little steps for me to focus on the next day. I will never forget her words. She wrote, 'Have a hot drink or some water, go to the doctor's and text your friend, Rob. Remember you are loved by so many people, take some 'me' time when it all gets too much. Love you Sis, sending you a big hug because I can't give you one in person.' It meant the world to me that Rosie could guide me through this dark time in my life. It is so important to have that one person that you can always turn to, anytime of day. Sarah and Kerry stood by my sides as we walked home, holding onto my arms. My breathing was laboured, as I looked at the ground and took that slow journey home.

The following day, I visited the family doctor who prescribed a low dosage of antidepressants and listened, shocked while I told her the whole story. Well, maybe not the whole story. It was a nice release talking to someone who was neutral because I could just let it all out, without any judgement whatsoever. When I got home, I had a very long sleep before writing an extensive to-do list, starting with sorting out my finances. The list included everything from finishing the kitchen renovations to allocating some housework to the kids. The list would give me something to focus on until Julian moved out, helping in my recovery.

As the weeks went by, I was torn between focusing on my wellbeing and surreptitiously checking Julian's laptop for evidence of pornography or dating websites. There were times when I thought I might be literally going crazy, repeatedly searching for anything that would ultimately cause more pain and harm to my wellbeing. I craved affection and wished that Julian was heterosexual, but deep down I knew he never was going to be, and we had different needs. For many years, I had been suppressing my emotions and desires and I realised that I needed more, much more than I had received in the marriage. I wanted a man to desire me in every way possible. I thought back to all the times I would dress up for special occasions and events, wearing a new dress, getting my hair and makeup done. Other people would notice and compliment my appearance, but Julian either said nothing or only commented when I asked him how I looked. In early 2015, I attended a friend's wedding with Julian, making a special effort to look nice, wearing a pretty blue dress and getting my makeup done professionally. The kids and my friends said I looked fantastic.

My friend Judy turned to Julian and said, 'Aren't you proud of how beautiful your wife looks today?'

CHAPTER 6

All he could say was 'Mm yes.' This reaction was typical and predictable, but I thought it would be nice, just once, for him to notice me and have an expression that showed that he was proud to be out with his wife. Surely, I was more than just a mother, friend and teacher; I was a woman, a sexual being with needs like other women.

It was no different to the first time I spent a night away with Julian, when we were just friends and getting to know each other. We booked a room at Sovereign Hill with two single beds and a lovely view of the lake. After an exciting day, riding on the horse and carriage, eating hard boiled lollies and having our palms read, it was getting dark outside, so we decided to return to our room. We took off our shoes and lay on our own beds talking about our families mostly. I smiled at Julian with that sultry look that means, 'I like you and would be happy if you kissed me right now.' He never moved an inch from his bed, just laughing at my jokes and agreeing with everything I said. I wanted to swiftly jump across to the other side of the room and kiss him, but in those days, I always believed it was the man who should make the first move. What if he did not like me in that way? I could not face the possible rejection, so I decided to get dressed for bed in the adjoining bathroom. We talked until the early hours of the morning, played a game of cards and sat close together. I enjoyed his company, hanging on his every word, fixated on his long, dark eyelashes. I smiled and moved in even closer, looking at his full lips in anticipation of a first kiss. He looked nervous, even child-like and proceeded to talk about our plans for the next day. We spoke for a while longer and I realised that there was not going to be any kiss, unless I initiated it myself and I was not going to do that. I felt disappointed, wondering whether he just did not find me attractive or maybe he was just inexperienced and did not know what to do. For the rest of the weekend, I remained more quiet than usual, afraid of what I may say. He just acted as usual, which agitated me even more. Later that week, I told Julian that it just wasn't working, and it was best that we did not continue with the relationship. His sister spoke to me and said that she thought he could possibly be asexual, and this made me think I had been too harsh on Julian. I missed his friendship and asked if he wanted to continue as friends. Julian said that he also missed spending time together and really enjoyed my company. I gave him a second chance to find out if we could develop our friendship. Julian's mum told me how he was devastated in the weeks that we were apart, moping around the house, singing love songs.

I always gave second chances, just as I did when we tried to make the marriage work after the disclosure. For the months that followed, I knew that whenever I left the house for any reason, he would hurriedly open his laptop to view pornography. I would not waste any time either checking his history, finding the usual sites of gay sex, hot males, large cocks and similar images.

Sometimes I did not even need to check because the signs were there in his appearance and reaction. The laptop would be out of the desk drawer, his face would be red, and he would appear tired. He had the audacity to complain about having to cook dinner or that he had so much preparation to do for work. He could have been more productive if he wasn't looking at disgusting videos of porn, which ultimately led to him falling asleep.

CHAPTER 7

Changes in appearance were starting to happen. Once Julian weighed over 80 kilograms, with a hairy chest and masculine body. He was now less than 70 kilograms, with a shaved chest, arms and pubic region. His clothing and appearance became more important to him than ever before. Tight fitted pants and shirts, bright coloured t-shirts and colourful loom bands on his wrist. A point of no return. A forty-eight-year-old man wanting to look twenty. I enquired, 'If you had a male partner one day, what age group would you prefer?'

He replied, 'About twenty-five or older.'

I was shocked, thinking how our eldest was twenty-one, instantly feeling sick and regretting that I had asked the question. My big mouth. My inquisitive nature. It was so challenging living together, knowing that my husband wanted a man, something I could never be. I still loved him, and it felt so unfair.

I started considering my future and what I really aspired to. What were my dreams? My dreams had always been to grow old with Julian, watch our children grow up, retire together, travel around Australia in a campervan and spend quality time with our future grandchildren. This plan was etched in my mind, but it could no longer be. I was still alive, there were many positives in my life, and I would focus on my children, family, friendships and my career. I had goals and milestones to reach and I would work tirelessly towards them. Later in the year I would start my creative nonfiction writing course at RMIT, hoping to eventually get my memoir published. I always enjoyed writing. My first piece was a thesis written at University about boys and how they learn best. Many years later I wrote my dear mother's history and compiled my uncles' war letters. Now the time was ripe for me to focus on my memoir. The writing course would hopefully assist me with structure and form. I had filled several exercise books with snippets of my life. Writing about my marriage, I could see how my fractured relationship with my father had an incredible effect on my choices in partners. Why was I spending my life avoiding anyone and anything that reminded me of him?

I had a ton of paperwork and phone calls to make to sort out the details of the separation. Once that was all finished, I decided I would concentrate once again on my recovery, starting those long-forgotten hobbies and catching up more with friends. My life could be whatever I imagined it to be if I just focused on my goals. In the next few years, I wanted to take yoga classes, dance classes, swimming lessons and singing tuition. Ultimately, I wanted to swim to keep fit and join a choir, but I had some work to do first. I would never be lonely when Julian moved out because I had a beautiful family, loyal friends and some new friends that I had met through the online Straight Spouse Support Group. One day I sincerely hoped to meet a man that would love me as I deserved with his whole heart.

Writing became my cathartic tool to cleanse myself of my negative, self-destroying emotions and it also gave me a focus other than my marriage breakdown. The closet that Julian had created for himself not only hurt him, but the kids and me as well. The anger, betrayal, shock and sadness was going to take months, if not years to recover from. I had trust issues and my energy levels were low most of the time. Boundaries and other changes needed to be made even before Julian moved out. I told him that I would not continue to walk every night with him, since this would not be possible once he no longer lived here. I could use this time to catch up with my friends. Julian and I spent the day in the city as we were on school holidays. It was now that I noticed Julian becoming increasingly defensive of gay people and anyone who might appear different. As we walked through the city, I noticed a man with extreme facial piercings and facial tattoos. I casually remarked that, 'I would never want a facial tattoo, especially that amount because it just does not look very nice.' Julian got defensive, stating that 'He is only expressing who he really is!' I had no issue with people being who they wished to be, but I was taken aback by his sudden change of heart towards tattoos. He used to openly hate them with a passion. He was changing in every way, his attitude, his clothes, jewellery and hair removal. Now he was not letting me have my own opinion if it was not in alliance with his own thoughts. I wasted no time in telling him that he had changed so much and not necessarily for the better.

Julian snapped, 'You should get used to the fact that people do change!'

I retorted, 'My general views have and never will change!' Typically, he brought the conversation back to himself and his revelation of being gay.

'Do you want to stay in a marriage that is not happy?' He rubbed salt in the wound by reminding me that my own mother stayed in her marriage even though it was not good for her or her kids. To rouse me even more he went further by asking, 'Would you be happy if I just ended my life?'

I could not believe the way he twisted a comment about tattoos to me wanting him to end his life. He was good at this technique of making himself the victim after the disclosure and the suffering endured by the kids and me. My opinion of him was diminishing as time went on. Earlier that day we visited the Art Gallery. I only went along because he had purchased the tickets many months before and did not want to waste money. Of course, I could not fully enjoy the experience of viewing De Gas's paintings and everything turned into an argument. I was becoming as hypersensitive as he was, annoyed at anything that reminded me of his betrayal or anything related to sex. One such instance was after reading a description of one of the paintings. The report explained how Vincent Van Gogh died of syphilis, the same artist that Julian held in such high regard. Julian always became emotional when he heard the song 'Starry Night,' droning on about how Vincent Van Gogh was misunderstood and a victim of societal expectations. This was most likely true, and he was a brilliant artist, but this did not stop me from saying 'Van Gogh died of a sexually related disease and maybe he was not all that innocent after all.'

Julian replied, 'His wife probably gave it to him!' I felt so outraged that he could blame a woman, as if it was women who caused all the pain and suffering in relationships. I took the whole conversation as a personal attack and the rage almost caused me to start pounding his chest, shouting, 'It's your fault, you and no one else!' Since it would not be appropriate in a public gallery, I retaliated by using words as my weapons, stating that 'Van Gogh must have visited a brothel and he got his just dessert.'

He retorted, 'Women are not perfect, and De Gas knew that, so he was a misogynist. He hated women.'

I had a strong feeling that this conversation was not going to end there, and it clearly was not going to end well. I surreptitiously glanced around the room to see if anyone was in earshot. My blood was boiling, and my face reddened as I turned to Julian and snapped, 'Well, why did he paint women all the time, especially his sisters? I heard he loved his sisters. Paintings of women sold very well in his time and he knew it. You have it all wrong! You are the only one that hates women!' I walked as fast I possibly could to the exit, almost knocking the security guard over as I stormed out. I practically ran to the city train station, as Julian followed behind me. He entered the carriage I was on, but I could not look at him. I wanted to cry, scream, run, just be anywhere but stuck on a train for half an hour with him.

CHAPTER 7

When we reached our station, I ran to the car, briskly climbing into the passenger seat, dreading the fifteen-minute drive from the station to my house. I glared stone-faced at Julian, 'I don't want you to end your life because it would affect the kids.' The small amount of love that I had for him was replaced by resentment, anger and disappointment. There was a time when I would have done almost anything for him, even put my own life at risk. I could not control my emotions, crying the entire journey. We blamed each other for the marriage breakdown, hurling insult after insult. He told me I was the controlling one, organising everything from what we ate to where we travelled. I retorted, stating that he was deceitful and indifferent, never caring enough to show affection. Julian banged his hands fiercely on the steering wheel, nearly causing an accident when we just managed to stop at the roundabout before a red Ford zoomed past. My heart was racing, and my eyes could not see through the cascade of tears. When we finally made it home, I raced into Sarah's room to escape from Julian. He was not the same person that I once loved with every ounce of my existence. He was a stranger, an adversary. Sarah looked awfully worried, asking what was wrong. I struggled to breathe, sobbing and gasping. She handed me some tissues and pleaded, 'Mum, what happened?' I told her that her Dad and I had an argument and he was driving dangerously. I told her that I hated him so much. Sarah hugged me, shaking her head.

CHAPTER 8

The front door slammed shut, causing the house to shake and I knew it would be Julian going for a walk to clear his head. After a few minutes, panic took over my body. Was Julian serious that he wanted to end his life? I started shouting out loud to no one in particular, ranting how I had to find him. 'It's my fault. It's my fault if anything bad happens.' 'I shouldn't have said anything; I should not have argued. It's my fault!' I grabbed the car keys, but Sarah snatched the keys from my hand, insisting that I did not get in the car.

'Please Mum, I will drive. You can't drive in this state!' Sarah was a learner driver, but it was better that she drove. My mind was racing, reflecting on every possible place that Julian could have walked to. I could not breathe again, as though all the air had been sucked out of me. Brandon and his friend John were in another car, also searching the typical places like the local park and shopping centres but to no avail. Sarah and I searched in similar areas, also stopping at the local creek. We had walked along this part of the creek as a family many times before, in much happier times. During the day the creek was serene, surrounded by beautiful Willow trees and native birds as diverse as the leaves on the trees. By now it was too dark to see anything, even my own feet in front of me. The ground was muddy, and the atmosphere felt unnerving as we walked a few metres closer to the murky water. I could hear myself screaming, 'Julian, Julian, Julian…' It was pointless, but I had to try, I had to let him know that I wanted him alive. There was no point staying here any longer and I did not want to put Sarah's life at risk. We drove a few blocks to the supermarket, running in to ask the friendly checkout lady, Jenny, if she had seen my husband in the last hour or so. Jenny's son, Eddie, used to be in the same class as Sarah in Year 10, so we knew each other. Jenny had been working for a few hours and had not seen him. I thanked her anyway and ran back to the car. We searched the local park again, surrounding streets and the nearest railway station. The Protective Services Officer at the station was most helpful, taking my number and promising to call me if he saw anyone fitting Julian's description. He was even willing to call other stations on the railway line to ask if they had noticed him. I could have hugged him at that moment. I rang everyone I could think of, including Julian's friend Rob, his sister Barbara and the police. Rob rang all the surrounding McDonalds, hoping he may have stopped to have a drink or go to the toilet.

Sarah and I retraced our steps again, as I prayed out loud. 'Please dear God, let him be safe. If we find him, I promise you God that I will not argue like that again. Please let him be alive and safe!' I knew that I could not live with myself if I caused Julian to end his life. I felt like everything was crumbling before my eyes. Brandon and Sarah reminded me that Julian was old enough to make his own decisions and that ultimately, I had no control over his decisions. Rob managed to calm my nerves by taking control and letting me know that I had done everything possible to find him. Sarah was my rock, comforting me with her words and advice. Although she was only nineteen, she was mature beyond her years and I had so much faith and trust in her. Although I desperately wanted to run out the door and keep searching the streets for Julian, Sarah's composure was the medicine I needed to stay put and just wait on his return.

Thankfully, Charlotte was in the city with friends, totally oblivious to the fact that her Dad had ran off.

Sarah agreed to drive around the block with me to search once more around the local streets. She looked at my face, covered with tears and runny mascara, 'Mum, after this you should rest and maybe let the Police look for Dad.' Sarah and I drove around our local area, gazing in the darkness at anything that resembled a person or even something that moved. It was after midnight and there were very few people on the streets. 'That's him!' After a closer look, it was obvious that the person appeared nothing like him. Feeling exhausted and hopeless, I knew that I would be more use at home resting, but I just wanted to check the local park one more time. Unsure whether my weary eyes were playing tricks again, I noticed a dark figure sitting on a bench with a familiar football beanie on his head. If it wasn't Julian, it was someone very similar. Who else would be sitting at a bench in the darkness at this hour wearing the same knitted beanie? After stopping the car, Sarah and I ran across the road toward the figure. I immediately knew it was Julian by the way he was walking away. He did not want to see us, but Sarah continued after him until he stopped. I kept my distance, watching helplessly as Sarah tried to get him to stop walking and to listen. My usual reaction would have been to rebuke Julian for putting his family through so much strain, but I remembered my promise to God. I hugged Julian, but he remained frozen and unresponsive. 'Come home Julian and we can talk. We have searched everywhere for you!'

Julian looked at the ground, whispering, 'I don't want to burden anyone, and I don't want to go home.' Sarah and I persisted and managed to get him in the car and finally back home.

I rang the Police to let them know Julian was safe, and they told me they would send some material to my house with numbers for advice and support. I rang his sisters to let them know he was home safe, and they were also relieved. Back home we all cried some more, through relief and frustration. I wondered how we would all get through this harrowing time and could not see a positive future, just darkness and pain. I told Julian he could not take off every time there was conflict or when things got too hard. Running away just made the problem worse. Julian explained that he walked for four hours, only stopping once to look for a diary at the supermarket and to go to the toilet. Ironically, he was at the supermarket only ten minutes after I spoke to Jenny, the checkout lady. She told him that I was looking for him. For the next few hours we lay in bed, finding it impossible to sleep. I told him that I didn't want any harm to come to him and he must believe that. I was thankful that he was alive, but the love I once had for him was now replaced by pity and a kind of bitterness. He had aged, was much thinner and very distant. Who was this man that I married all those years ago? I continued to write down my feelings and thoughts, as it alleviated my mind and helped me to focus on the positive moments in each day, as scarce as they were at times. I wished that I could let my other family members know what was going on, but I didn't know how they would react or cope. We had to learn how to cope, before letting others know. The 'closet' continued to hurt us all, placing the kids and me in a precarious position of keeping a secret that made our lives one big lie. I felt trapped, in shock, even catatonic at times. The betrayal, anger, fear and rage just sat in the pit of my stomach like a dormant volcano, ready to erupt at any point. The children and I were collateral damage of a situation that was in no way our fault and in which we had no control over. Our family was destroyed! I promised God to be patient with Julian, but daily I just wanted to scream, 'Why the fuck did you do this to us?' He certainly did have a choice! I am not a cure for gayness! Why didn't he pick on someone else? I thought to myself, I may be too old now to ever experience real love again with a man who would truly love me as a woman. I needed a recovery plan. Plans always worked for me before in other aspects of my life, like work or for my fitness. The first step was recovery. Recovery from the pain, heartache, sorrow, loss of dreams. Only then would I be able to rediscover myself as an independent, single mother. What did I want in my future? I wanted a lot of things, peace, love, music, hobbies, friendship and security.

CHAPTER 9

Julian wanted to remain good friends for the rest of our lives. What does that even mean? How can an ex-husband become a friend? I was not sure how this would be possible, when I had no trust or faith in anything he said. Julian rarely answered his phone when we needed him. Did I really want a friend like that? Time was my best friend. He was certainly being generous financially by paying for the kitchen renovations and suggesting that I keep the house and car. Discussions about the house, finances and other matters could wait. All I really wanted was a secure place for the kids and I to live.

It was ironic that in the last twelve months, the media was inundated with debates about legalising same-sex marriage. Would Julian want to marry a man one day, after the divorce and once he found a partner? My mind went straight to the legalities if gay marriage became legal. Could Julian's future partner make a claim on our house, when we always agreed that the house would be left to the children? I had to protect the house and myself, deciding to see a solicitor in the next few months. There was no way on Earth that I was going to lose the house that we had worked so hard towards.

Julian was becoming increasingly moody as the months rushed by and the moving date was fast approaching. He was impatient with the kids, often getting into arguments over trivial matters, like dirty dishes, and he often misinterpreted their intentions. He was often distant and in his own little world, almost like a ghost in the house, existing but not really interacting. He was searching up gay pornography on a regular basis, whenever the opportunity arose. Although we were living under the same roof and separated, it felt like he was rubbing salt in the wound every time he watched pornography. I felt disgusted, knowing that every time I went out, he would jump on to the laptop to get his rocks off, in a manner of speaking. His computer history disclosed how often he was watching young, virile men with unrealistic erections and fortitude, screwing each other or sucking

CHAPTER 9

on gargantuan penises. I had no power to prevent him from looking, he was addicted to porn and absurdly I was now addicted to checking if he was still watching it. I loathed myself for checking for two reasons. Firstly, because I was invading his privacy, but mainly because what I discovered only reinforced the fact that Julian never loved me in the way that I always believed and his passion would always lie with men, especially young, virile ones. I detested those abhorrent sites, deeming them as my opposition, the reason for all this treachery and unfaithfulness. I resented the sight of his oversized old, black laptop in the living room, as I knew it meant it was not used for work purposes, like the newer one. The smaller laptop was for his work, so I never felt compelled to check that one. I contemplated expediently throwing the laptop out of the window and smashing it to a billion pieces, but what would that solve? There were other laptops he could use, and he could also use his phone or read magazines.

At the same time, Julian's elderly mother, Maria was still now terminally ill, unconscious of the fact that her 'perfect' son was not the model husband and father that she always believed him to be. Two of Julian's sisters were at Maria's unit when we visited that week, very sympathetic to how tough the separation was for both of us during this challenging period. They were understanding of both sides and I appreciated their kindness and their unbiased attitude. As I held Maria's tiny hand, I wondered if she would have accepted Julian's coming out. It would only be a week later that Maria would pass away after months of lying in her bed, holding onto life. She was so small and fragile at the end. It was a distressing week, dealing with the loss of Maria, while still coming to terms with our dissolving marriage. During the funeral and the lead up to it, I suppressed my emotions to be a support and comfort to Julian and his family, just as he supported me when my dear mother passed away two years earlier. It was the right thing to do and I did feel part of his family for so many years, but it felt hypocritical acting as the adoring wife. At the funeral, as I stood next to him greeting family and friends, some who still had no idea that we were not together, I felt like a phoney. I looked and dressed the part of the mourning wife, but I knew this would not be my family for much longer. I felt deeply sad for the loss of Maria, who gradually welcomed me into her big European family, accepting me as another daughter. My grief was deepened by the knowledge that my husband never loved me in the way that I had loved him. I resented him for his deceit. I resented the fact that his family would no longer be mine. I tried not to show my grievance to the other mourners, but I guess we were all too sad to notice much else any way. I wondered if this is how those people in the public eye must have felt when their partner was having an affair. People like Jacky Kennedy and Lady Diana, who played their part for the public, but inside they were possibly just holding it together. If it appeared that we were a happy, loving couple, then everything would be fine, at least for now. Inside I was fuming, desperately wanting to scream out the words in my head, 'He is not the perfect man that you all think he is. He is a liar, a fraud, he is gay. I don't want to be here right now. Get me out of here! Please let me fall into a giant hole, anywhere but here!'

As time went on, we all needed something positive to focus on after such a trying year. I joined a local yoga group, on my path to gaining some 'me' time and rediscovering what I wanted in my life at fifty years old. I thought yoga would be an ideal hobby to help me relieve tension, relax and possibly meet new friends. What I didn't know was that the yoga group was an advanced class and the movements were so arduous I felt stressed and self-defeated. The instructor always targeted me, repeating 'This is the correct way! For you, just try this part.' It was evident to me and everyone else in the class that I would never be able to master the moves. I persevered for three long, painstaking weeks, dreading every class until I concluded that it was not for me.

It was six months since the revelation. I felt defeated, drained emotionally and physically. Julian was pretty much the same. The night after Julian's mother's funeral we were so heartbroken that we held on to each other the entire night. Julian began kissing me on the lips and I responded unwittingly, not pausing to consider what it might lead to. He gently caressed my breasts while we kissed, and I rubbed his penis. It felt amazing, I desperately longed for this closeness and passion. For a fleeting moment, I hoped that he could change his mind about his sexuality, but I knew deep down that this would be the last time that we would ever be this physically close again. As expected, the following day Julian was back on his laptop browsing the usual pornographic sites at every possible moment. I could never compete with something as powerful as the Internet, nor would I want to try.

The following week, Julian's younger brother, nephew and two great nephews arrived in a truck with his mother's old furniture. Julian would use it to furnish his new unit. There was a small fridge, single bed, antique dresser and a small, rectangular dining table, amongst other bits and pieces. It took all my resolve to hold back my tears, as I walked past them to the car. I mumbled a quick hello as I walked impulsively to the car, barely out of the street when a flood of emotions swept over my body. The tears just kept coming and coming, as I sobbed uncontrollably. I struggled to see as I drove, so I pulled over to the side of the road. It felt the same as when I had read that letter that he handed me eight months earlier. The reality of the move was finally sinking in. I wiped the tears away and blew my painfully red nose. Was Julian feeling the same or was he looking forward to finally moving? I drove towards the local shops, taking a deep breath, reminding myself to take it all one day at a time as I usually did. Charlotte and I had a Michael Jackson tribute concert to attend in the evening and I was looking forward to the distraction. It was a fun night with Charlotte, the singer sounded exactly like MJ and even danced like him, but up close he obviously looked much different. We sang and danced the night away. Rosie texted me to see how the concert was and how I was going. I felt blessed to have my sister, friends and support group to get me through another testing part of the journey.

CHAPTER 10

Celebrations came and went throughout the year. The five of us all went out to a pizza restaurant for Julian's 48th birthday, where I composed myself and acted as if everything was normal, knowing that this would possibly be the last one we celebrated together, apart from the kids' birthdays. I would not be organising his next birthday, considering we would no longer be living together and that he might have a partner by then. I wondered whether I would ever meet someone. Who knows? I felt stressed about my upcoming fiftieth birthday, knowing that my family and Julian's family would be there, and it would be another event where I would have to appear happy and act naturally as if everything was still the same. I wanted to run away and hide in a cave until

I felt better again. I was not coping with work. I was not coping with home. I guess I was just not coping with life. Everyone and everything annoyed me, and nothing gave me any pleasure anymore. I turned the radio on, since music was the one thing that could usually lift my mood. The singer hummed, 'I would give everything I own, just to have you back.' I wanted desperately for Julian to feel this way, but the chances of that happening were as good as impossible.

I did what I usually did when I was stressed. Cleaned. I cleaned out the walk-in wardrobe; a sea of memories. I gathered all of Julian's belongings and placed them one by one in a large box. I stumbled upon the wedding album and other family photos, filled with over twenty years of memories. As I scanned the pages of memories, I felt my chest tightening and my face becoming flushed with anger. What was real? Was anything genuine? I looked for any possible sign in the photos, examining every photo like a private investigator. Was the man in the photos really the same man who was causing me so much pain and heartache? The man in the photo loved me with all his heart. He promised me that we would be together forever. He was my world, my everything. But he was just a hologram, a projected image. I saw what I was supposed to see and for me this was real. I tortured myself, scrutinizing every photo, twenty years of memories, searching for answers. Those dark eyes, long eyelashes and well-trimmed beard. I was not quite sure what I was looking for, but the process was causing even more pain. I decided to pack the photos in the box to deal with another time. I thought of ripping the photos or even burning them, but I knew if I did, there would be no way of getting them back if I somehow changed my mind.

Living together as a separated couple was soul destroying as our relationship continued to become more toxic. It felt as if I was dying slowly on the inside, like a shiny apple with a rotten core. Julian justified the lies and emotional abuse over the years, by saying that he could not change who he was. He repeatedly told me he was gay, and nothing was ever going to change that! Each day, I became more physically and emotionally exhausted, dependant on antidepressants to help me survive the day, knowing the future was so uncertain.

My birthday was fast approaching, and my emotions were increasingly changing with every day that passed. Sad, happy, uninterested, sad again. I was looking forward to seeing my family, but I was so tired of the pretence that I was doing well when I felt like I was drowning slowly. Julian made the cake and it was beautiful as usual, layers of chocolate cake and decorative icing. I was constantly worried how I would cope financially after we officially separated and how I would tell the rest of my family and friends. My trepidation felt like a mountain was about to crush me.

I turned to my Facebook support group for help. They were looking for volunteers to participate in a television program about people who divorce later in life. Initially the program wanted a few couples to discuss the reasons for the breakdown of their marriages. They agreed to talk to the straight partners and get their side of the story. About a week before production, the producer informed the participants that they wanted both sides of the story. This infuriated those that agreed to speak out because there was absolutely no chance that the gay ex-partner would agree to it. This was an opportunity for us to finally have a say on how our partner's coming out affected us and our children. There are already countless television programs that discuss the impact on the LGBTI community when they disclosed their sexuality. What about the straight partner? What about the affected children? We are forced into the closet too; we are forced to be silent and we are cheated on and abused. It was just not fair.

As the 'straight spouse' we are faced with abandonment, loss of dreams, an altered future, deceit and mostly self-doubt. I became Julian's beard, an object to hide behind for fear of being found out. He has his children now and the chance to meet the man of his dreams. The children and I will always be the collateral damage, dealing with the consequences and recurring nightmare that it is. How many future generations will have to deal with the same issues? The recovery process is truly like a roller coaster, filled with emotions and the ripple effects invade the lives of the partner, children, extended family and friends. Julian once told me, 'I love you, but not in the way you deserve.' It was supposed to make me feel better, but it just made me feel worse, unloved, used and abused. I asked him, 'Why now? Why the fuck now?' He looked down at the floor before looking at me like a dog that had just destroyed a favourite toy. 'I just could not stand it anymore, lying to you when you just didn't deserve it!' I wondered whether the timing of his 48th birthday was a mid-life crisis. Nearly fifty and there was still time to fulfil his dreams. He didn't want a sports car or a sexy young woman, he wanted a man. He always did want a man. What a nerve he had, revealing this secret and changing my destiny forever. Marriage was supposed to be forever, at least I married for love, I gave my heart, soul and everything else I had to this 'marriage'. I never held a gun to his head. I believed that he was heterosexual. How can I ever fully trust another man again, with the scars, the pain, the fear? My heart now has bars around it. It would take a special man to break through the barriers. I need to be cautious in case it happens all over again.

I thank God, that Julian did not have sex with men during the marriage. I may have contracted an STI or other infections, like many others have in similar circumstances. The innocent partner should have a right to sue them to cover the medical expenses and for the degradation. It just enrages me to no end that society is expected to embrace the whole 'coming out' process or we are labelled as old-fashioned, uncaring, even homophobic. I never considered myself homophobic, even when my parents told me it was unnatural, disgusting and against God. I was accepting of everyone, but now I looked at gays and lesbians with suspicion, analysing their motives. Some may call me a bigot or homophobic, but I just needed time to get over my hurt. I found it hard to trust anyone who was not straight. I remember my mum detesting Germans because of her two brothers dying in World War II. Her judgement was clouded by fear and hatred, yet it conflicted with my core belief that everyone deserved to be treated with respect and dignity. Did I really despise all gay people or was it only those that lied and deceived others? If I saw two guys walking down the street holding hands, I would quickly look away. I did not like myself at all for reacting this way, but the pain was too much to bear. This year had been so negative in so many ways and I was determined to achieve something positive out of all this misery. My story is not unique and there are thousands of others who face similar battles. I want to help people to break free from being trapped in a mixed–orientation marriage. I want to warn those that think they can somehow change their sexual preference by marrying into a heterosexual relationship. It never works! It never will! The partners and children are impacted forever, regardless of whether the separation is relatively amicable as mine was. The emotional abuse might not be obvious during the marriage until the separation. It becomes a normal part of life, weighing you down until you feel defeated and it became the norm. Julian's frustration of playing his role, mounted up over the years to the point of taking it out on the children and myself.

About 5 years earlier, I asked Julian why he never wanted to make love to me. He replied, 'If you were just nicer, I might want to be more affectionate towards you and may even want to have sex!' I remember feeling my breath racing as I snapped, 'How dare you place all the blame on me, when I am only angry because of the way you treat me!' I told a close friend and she said that she had never met a nicer and more accommodating person as myself. Even still, I started to believe everything he told me, feeling trapped in a loveless marriage. I became a little bitter towards him as the years progressed, bitter towards life.

I felt unloved.

Neglected.

Ignored.

Shunned.

Invisible.

An invisible bystander in a fake marriage. For the second half of the marriage, Julian would retire to bed very early, ensuring that he was fast asleep before I retired to bed. I asked him now and then why he always went so early. He replied, 'I am so tired after a hard day at work and I need to get up early to fit in exercise before work.' I was never an early riser, at least not as early as 4.30am like him. This was the reason that I had no clue that he was getting up early to take his laptop to the lounge room to look at those pictures and videos.

When I got into bed, he would be fast asleep, snoring. Occasionally he would roll over to give me a quick peck on the cheek. A peck that I commonly referred to as a 'grandma kiss.' His response to this was that he was just not like other men and I could take it or leave it. When we first married, he was more affectionate, even doting over me, especially when I was pregnant. This changed over time and his warmth declined, just as the marriage eventually would. I wondered whether the initial love and affection was just an act or did age influence his sex drive. I knew deep down that the former was most likely true, but I clutched on to straws to keep it all together.

CHAPTER 10

About half way through that year after the revelation I was feeling drained, depleted of energy and teary. I made an appointment with the doctor to renew my prescription for anti-depressants. Those tiny yellow pills helped take away some of the pain, although I was holding in my emotions most of the time. I never liked to show my weaknesses. I was the strong one who could cope with anything, or so I thought. I cried daily, asking Julian questions to see if he was feeling the same sort of turmoil. When I asked how he was feeling he often said nothing. This killed me. One day he told me he would rather not reply because he might offend me with his answer. We were still living together until the end of the year and this was the most challenging and wounding part of the journey, living with someone you once loved, possibly still did, only to see that they were not that person. He was a ghost. When he saw my tears, he said, 'I am glad that I met you and I don't regret having the children. I never meant to hurt you.' It sounded so final and only added salt to my wounds. We agreed to be friends forever. I wondered whether he would find a partner, considering his shyness. There was a tiny part of me that hoped he would come back one day, only to realise that he could not live without me and that he had made a big mistake. I must be in denial, hoping that his love for me was greater than his need to be with a man. I did not realise that his so-called love for me was his need for me to be happy and to find someone that could love me as a woman and fulfil my needs. He desperately wanted to be with a man, and this would always be his focus. Sometimes I wished that it would all blow up in his face, realising that even a man could not make him happy. Maybe he would realise that the grass isn't always greener on the other side.

CHAPTER 11

As much as I tried, I could not stop looking at his miserable laptop, obsessed with knowing what he was viewing when I left the house or was busy doing chores. One such site was 'How can you tell if a man is gay?' It annoyed me tremendously that he would be looking at this while we still lived together, but I guess that never hindered him before. He seemed to want to find someone and move on so quickly, while I was still mourning the marriage. I stupidly questioned him about it, and he sarcastically answered, 'Well, yes, you are perfect, and I am not! I will not deny that I am interested in men. Do you want me to live a lie? Is that what you really want Leanne?' He even went on to tell me that I at least knew what it was like to have a man when I had him, but he never got to experience this. He retorted, 'You must hate all men!' for telling him that he was 'never really a man in the true sense.' I could not believe that he was blaming me. Again. How dare he say I hated all men?! Right then I hated one man only. I was not sure how I could ever trust another man again. How would I know if he was telling the truth? How would I know if he really liked women? Would I forever be second guessing his motives? At this moment, I doubted whether I even wanted Julian as a friend. Friends are supposed to make you feel better about yourself but in the last few months we had spat some pretty nasty words at each other. Hurtful words. He truly believed that I would try to stop him from having a relationship in the future. There were no more words. My face was flushed with anger. I could not control his life and I did not want to either. His words were like a sharp knife, ripping pieces from my heart. There were four long months left until he moved out and it felt like an eternity. I was tired, dead tired of the arguments. Tired of his reactions. Tired of the constant reminder that my marriage was a sham. His coldness towards me increased like an endless snow storm as the weeks passed. I wanted to distance myself from any interaction with him. I planned to catch up with family and friends more, believing if I kept my distance that my pain would dissipate.

CHAPTER 11

To pass the time, I continued to sort through the wardrobe, separating out Julian's belongings. I came across photos of our family holidays when the children were small. A family unit, swimming at the beach, pushing the kids on the swings and standing proud at their school graduations. I stumbled across some older cream coloured photo albums that I had never seen before. I curiously opened one of them, noticing the photos were of Malta, most of them photos of his cousins and aunties. Some of them showed the grief and despair of the time when Julian's father passed away. The second album was a lot larger and kept in pristine condition. I had never seen this album before. The first page held photos of his family, mostly his mum and his brothers and sisters. There were more photos that I discovered as I flipped the pages. Photos of another man in his twenties, Maltese looking with a beard. In every photo, he was standing next to Julian, rather closely too. They were both about the same height, olive skin and wore almost identical checked flannelette shirts, the kind that farmers often wore. I remember seeing this man in a photo once before. His name was Philip and he was apparently Julian's best friend when he was in his early twenties. I did not know a great deal about him, only that they went everywhere together and one day they had a falling out. I found out a few weeks after Julian's coming out that he was more than a friend, he was also Julian's lover. I slowly turned over the pages of the album, studying each picture to look for any signs on his face. Was he in love with him? Did they look like friends? I could not really tell, except for Julian's embarrassed smile when they were in photos and no one else was in them. It killed me to think that many of the photos were taken at Sovereign Hill, a place that was supposed to be our special place, a place so close to where we married. When he took me there, was he trying to relive the times that they spent together? I could not look at them anymore, bawling and angry that those photos were placed next to our family ones. I stormed into the lounge room, telling him angrily that I did not want any photos of his boyfriend in the house. He said nothing. I told him to tell the kids that I loved them, taking off for an hour, sobbing and walking so fast that I had to sit down at the park bench. My eyes ached and I was so thirsty, wishing I had brought my drink bottle and tissues with me when I left so abruptly. I had my mobile phone with me but nothing else. He did not try to contact me, even though I had been gone for over an hour. When I got home, I told him how deeply hurt I was finding those photos. He showed no sympathy, answering back, 'Don't you get it, I AM GAY! I made one mistake twenty-one years ago. I made a mistake by marrying you! I may as well kill myself.' His face got redder with each painful word that he hissed, leaning closer to my face. Before I could reply he banged his fist on the kitchen bench, grabbed his favourite beanie and stormed out the front door. I was frightened that he might do something stupid, so I ran after him. Charlotte followed behind me. He was no longer in the court.

As we ran after him down the nearby grim lane way, he ran so fast that we lost sight of him. It was almost dark, the streetlights so dimly lit that it was impossible to go any further. We headed back home to get the car. I drove around the local streets, searching for any sign of him. His beanie. The dark grey coat. But there was nothing. After a few hours, I rang the police. He did not take his wallet or phone. Some of the kids' friends came over to help.

Sarah's friend Laura made me a cup of tea, trying to convince me that this was not my fault. I blamed myself. Maybe I should not have told him how I felt when I saw the photos…. Maybe I should not have spoken to him at all about anything. I had promised God that I would not fight with him anymore and now I had broken that promise. Julian was a walking time bomb, so it was only a matter of time before he exploded. I spoke to my sister, Rosie, and my Facebook support group. They helped me immensely, offering valuable support and advice. They said it wasn't my fault and that I was not responsible for his actions. If he was going to do anything, it would be his choice, not mine. I was grateful for the support, but I still felt horrible, believing it was my fault. I should have said nothing about the photos. I could have just packed them away and shut my mouth. Hours felt like days as the time ticked away. It was almost midnight when I heard a knock at the door, hoping he would walk in, sorry for his actions. It was Brandon's friend, John, who had also been out looking for Julian earlier. John had seen someone walking towards our house from the laneway towards our court, but it was hard to tell if it was him. Hesitant to walk this short route at this late hour, I jumped in the car with Sarah. As we drove around the corner, I could see a figure in the darkness, walking swiftly from the laneway. His walk was familiar, one leg straight while the other was slightly inward. He noticed us but kept on going. We followed him back home, where he walked like a zombie out the back door and under the pergola, ignoring everyone. He did not want to talk to anyone, but Sarah was able to convince him to talk to her. I sat solemnly on the couch with Brandon, resting my head on his strong shoulder. He hugged me tightly and told me it would all be fine now. I was not so sure, staring at the television but not hearing or seeing anything. There were no more tears to cry, no more words to say. I felt numb, lifeless and had no idea how I could ever talk to this 'stranger' again. It felt like hours later when Sarah came inside to see how I was.

She told me that Julian was not angry at me, he said that I deserved so much better than him. I suddenly realised that I had been looking at everything wrong. I had been mourning what was, instead of dreaming of a better future. It was time to move on, one day at a time. My marriage was over, and I had to stop searching for answers that were there all along. We agreed to try our best to get along for the kids' sake as well as our own. The stress had taken its toll on us both, causing us to lose weight and feel exhausted most of the time. It was a relief to focus on work, at least while I was there, I could forget about the living hell my home life felt like.

Julian placed some furniture and belongings in storage containers, and it felt somewhat better knowing I could start redecorating my bedroom to make it more of my own. The walls were full of memories, family photos, gifts and a well-worn bedspread that would soon be replaced by a fresh modern one. Decorating my room would be the first step to letting go of the past. I had been holding onto those last threads, but they were now broken, and my only choice was to start over.

It would be Father's Day soon. Over the last 21 years, I would always plan a special day for Julian, somewhere special for the five of us to celebrate as a family. Since our fathers had both passed away, he was treated like a king with all the attention focused on him for the day.

This year we would simply go out for lunch, the rest would be up to the kids. This would be the last Father's Day that we would celebrate together as a family. One of many 'lasts.' Later that night, Julian and I stayed up late to speak about old times, the special places we had visited with the children, like the historical Sovereign Hill and Torquay, swimming all day and the long beach walks at night. We cried, knowing that these holidays were little gems in a marriage filled with sadness and regrets. We told each other that we would support each other in any way if we ever needed anything. It was so painful to think of all the lasts, whether it be Christmas, Easter, birthdays or just every day occurrences that we often took for granted. Julian said he might be making the biggest mistake of his life; however, he was still getting up early every morning and opening his laptop to watch explicit sex scenes between two, three or more men. I could not live like this much longer. The turmoil and confusion were causing me to lose weight, catch colds and suffer from unbearable headaches daily. I no longer could keep his secret from the rest of my family when they wondered why they had not heard from me for a long time. The reaction was always the same.

No way, I can't believe it.
Is he sure?
Maybe it's a phase

CHAPTER 12

No phase would last that long. He was always gay and only now was he accepting that. Only now was I accepting it. As problematic as it was to live with a husband who was same-sex attracted, I believed that I was no longer in love with him. He had never been true to himself. His lies were now out in the open and it was he who must deal with the consequences. His hair and beard were looking greyer than I remember and there were more lines around his eyes and on his forehead. His face was much thinner, drawn, revealing hollow cheek bones. His efforts to look more attractive, lifting weights and taking vitamins were not revealed in his appearance. It was obvious that he was trying to look younger to attract a man, but it was possible that he was trying all too hard.

The moment I thought I was coping better, I would be triggered by something in the media. Television shows and movies were jammed pack with scenes of males kissing or coming out. I felt nauseous and constantly reminded that I never really had the love that I always craved for in my marriage. I needed to get away, to collect my thoughts so I decided to stay with my sister, Grace, for the night. My three sisters and I spent the night at Grace's, reminiscing about old times and laughing like we hadn't for a long time. My older sisters were so supportive, letting me know that they would always be there for me. It felt cathartic and relaxing after explaining how I first felt when Julian told me and how I was dealing with the enforced changes. We played cards and other games, watched videos and ate junk. The next day my brothers-in-law arrived to pick up my sisters and I noticed that they hugged and kissed them as soon as they walked in the door. Watching the love and affection between each couple, I realised that I had never experienced that same kind of response. I had an aching need to be deeply loved, to be treasured in this way. Would I ever find a man that loved me in this way, someone who would walk on hot coals for me? Dating was perplexing and a process that I was not looking forward to, but I had to start one day if I was ever going to share my life with a loving man. I wondered if I would have to separate the wheat from

CHAPTER 12

the chaff, the frogs from the princes. At fifty years old, I did not want to date anyone who was younger than forty-five or older than fifty-five, reducing my prospective partners to those who were mostly divorced or widowed. There would certainly be baggage, and I had more than my fair share to bring to a relationship.

I returned home to a loving welcome from my kids. They jumped out of their seats to hug me and tell me how much they missed me. I had missed them too. Julian was very formal, just saying, 'Hello.' He had that all so familiar look in his eyes, tired and worn out with a hint of guilt. His personal laptop was closed next to him as he lay on the couch. I did not need to guess what he had been doing that afternoon. As soon as he arose to go to the toilet and the door shut, I hurriedly and ashamedly opened the lid of the laptop, pressed the History tab and observed the longest list I had witnessed of male pornography and same-sex dating sites. I felt sick in my stomach once again but knew I must stop checking. This would be the very last time.

In the next few days, we sought a solicitor to assist us in managing our property settlement. There were a few recommendations from friends and work colleagues, but unfortunately, we decided on the cheapest one. When we arrived at the front, the building looked like an old house, set in an impoverished suburban area. There was no one supervising the front desk, but within minutes a scruffy looking man dressed in old jeans and a stretched grey windcheater, resembling a cleaner, came out of a side door and told us to sit down in the plain, shabby waiting room. He proceeded to bring a small card table out from the room and placed it in the middle of the waiting room right in front of us, introducing himself as the solicitor and asked how he could help. As people walked in and out the front entrance, I felt awkward, speaking quietly to the old man, stating that we needed advice on how to draw up a legally binding agreement. He spoke in legal jargon throughout the conversation, confusing us both even further. He referred us to Relationships Australia Victoria and told us we must get separate solicitors. I called the next day, but they were also no help at all, so I decided to make a list of all the local solicitors and look at their reviews online.

Meanwhile my coordinator at work, referred me to a counsellor through our head office. I was entitled to five appointments, free of charge. I hesitantly agreed and booked a session. The counsellor spoke with a foreign accent and I struggled to understand her, but on the first visit she mainly listened and nodded, writing down everything I said. She mainly focused on things like how many siblings I had and what number I was in the family. The second visit was perturbing and one that I do not think I will ever forget. The very first thing she told me was that my husband would have felt repulsed when he had sex with me because I was a woman and not a man. I started crying, saying 'Well, he should not have married me then!' She also said it was unfair of me to say that I wished that I had a man that could truly love me when I was unhappy for him to seek a male partner. I just stayed quiet the rest of the session, not listening, just waiting for the time to hit 2pm so I could leave. When I reached my car, I just sat and bawled my eyes out, doubting myself and feeling worse than I had in a long time. Was the counsellor gay as well? Was she biased for some other reason? I wanted to run away and clear my head. I drove home sobbing the whole journey. As soon as I got home, Julian asked how it went. I just asked him, 'Did you feel repulsed when we made love? This is what the horrid counsellor said to me.' Julian told me that she was very unprofessional, and he was never repulsed. He said that she should never have said such nasty, incorrect things to me, especially after everything I had been through already in the past months. He hugged me tight, the way he did when Mum passed away.

    The next day I did not go to work. My head was throbbing, and I needed to see my regular counsellor instead. She listened to my complaints about the other counsellor that work recommended, commenting that people like her give the profession a bad name and that there are good and bad people in all professions. It helped me to gain my confidence back again and to put effort into the upcoming week. My wonderful son, Brandon turned twenty-one and we celebrated with family and friends at home. It was such a fantastic evening, with the party finishing about 4.30am. Everyone danced, both young and old, strutting their stuff to eighties music, modern songs and the classics like the 'Bus Stop' and the 'Macarena.' To make the week even more special, Brandon got his driver's licence and his beloved Bulldogs won the AFL Grand Final. We managed to put our worries behind us and enjoy the week of celebrations.

I wondered what the future birthday parties would be like once Julian moved out into his unit. There were only three months left and there were countless more celebrations leading up to our separation. It always felt awkward because Julian and I needed to appear like a happily married couple, while we were simply counting the days until the removal truck would turn up. Our youngest, Charlotte, finished Year 12 and Julian and I attended the Graduation ceremony. Most of the parents were unaware that Julian and I were not together anymore. We walked in as parents, no holding hands like many others. We sat in the overcrowded theatre, watching proudly as the students gathered on the stage in their formal gowns to receive their certificates. I felt distant from Julian, no longer able to grip hands or gaze into each other's eyes like we did when they received awards in their younger years. He hardly spoke, the lady next to me spoke more than he did. He never really liked to socialise anyway, preferring his own company or that of only close family.

When it was time to move out into the foyer to congratulate the students, Julian wanted to wait outside. I was surprised, encouraging him to stay and see his daughter and her friends and give them our best wishes. He reluctantly stayed, standing in the corner as I hugged Charlotte and her close friends. I realised even more how different we were. In the past, I would have agreed and waited outside to keep the peace, but I was getting stronger and becoming my own person again.

CHAPTER 13

The Legal Binding Agreement was taking forever to complete, waiting for Julian to visit his solicitor to get the papers signed. It was frustrating, I never asked for this separation and ironically, I was the one having to organise solicitors and paperwork. I wrote a list for Julian with step-by-step instructions of what he had to do. I was not dictating to him, just reminding him of what we had discussed. He could be a little too relaxed when it came to organising anything, whether it was appointments, outings, parties or holidays. I remember back to our first date. We had organised to meet at a certain place near the railway station. I must have waited for half an hour before I rang his sister on one of those old pay phones. She told me he had left, so I looked around and wondered if he misunderstood my instructions. After calling his sister a second time, I discovered that he was waiting on the other side of the station. There were no mobile phones then, so I decided to walk through the dark and dirty underpass to meet him on the other side. But as I crossed the road at the lights, I heard a horn beeping; he was driving past. We eventually met up, but by then I was frozen cold and a little annoyed. This type of confusion recurred over and over throughout the marriage, causing countless misunderstandings and arguments, especially considering how ordered I like my life to be.

Another occasion plays on my mind. We went to a concert without the children. It was a rare event to go out together alone, unless it was to a funeral or another more sombre occasion. Julian bought tickets for a concert and it meant a lot to me because we both liked this artist and his music. I thought it would be a great opportunity to have some quality time together, assuming it would somehow make us closer and possibly even more intimate. I bought a new dress and took extra time and effort on my makeup and waving my hair. My son, Brandon commented, 'You look really nice tonight Mum.' I thanked him, pausing to see if Julian would say the same. He mumbled something to the effect of 'That colour really suits you.' I guess I did not expect anymore, but I always remained hopeful.

CHAPTER 13

The concert hall was packed, with many couples holding hands and demonstratively displaying their love for each other. I sat in my seat, swaying and singing to the music, as Julian sat almost motionless staring towards the stage. Where was the connection between us? There was none. Although my stomach was churning and I felt like crying, I unreservedly focused on the stage as well. One of our favourite songs was played, one that reminded us of each other, but again he showed no hint of emotion or even a hint of affection. Was I so unworthy of love? What was wrong with me?

After the disclosure and whilst still living together, Julian precipitously wanted to go on many more outings together, more than we ever had in our entire marriage. Why now? We went for long walks along the beach or the local creek. He took me out for dinner, reaching out to me more than ever. It would be a gross understatement to say I was a little confused. My emotions were everywhere, crying one day and elated the next. Here was my husband, that I had loved unequivocally for many years, showing me another side to him now that we were in the process of separating. I still loved him, and I was holding onto hope for any sign that we may get back together. I may have been delusional at the time, but my emotions were all over the place and I was not my usual self, in fact, I did not know who I was anymore.

As we planned the final move, I made a point of suggesting that we set boundaries with each other for when we lived apart. He often spoke about being my 'best friend for life,' and that I would be the only woman he would ever love in his life time. If this was supposed to make me feel any better, it failed dismally. I may have fallen out of love but I had feelings for him, and emotions were not like a tap that you could just turn off, as much as I wished I could. He may have perceived me as his bestie, but I was not at the same stage. We made an agreement that Julian would occasionally come over on a Saturday to do some gardening, as it was way too much on my own and I never was much of a gardener. We would possibly catch up for coffee with the kids, but not on our own, not while we were trying to get used to being single and starting our new lives. Obviously, the kids could visit him as often as they wanted. There were a few months left before the final move and I initiated plans to catch up with friends and family more often to keep myself busy.

I wanted to go out and socialise not only to reconnect with friends, but also to shift my thinking patterns from a married woman to one who had a whole new future ahead of her. The first outing would be with my eldest daughter Sarah and her friend to the movies. I dressed up in new jeans and a pretty orange-red blouse. Julian looked up from the couch with a captivated look on his face. He said that I looked particularly nice this evening. Why didn't he ever say these things to me while we were together? Perhaps he was scared that it may lead to intimacy and I could get the wrong idea. I would never really know, but it was pointless to keep going over it. The horse had already bolted.

Our financial future needed to be sorted out with our respective solicitors before Christmas. His solicitor kept delaying proceedings, the latest excuse being that he did not believe in Financial Binding Agreements since they don't hold up well in court. To add even more stress, Julian was not trying very hard to find a unit. It was not my responsibility to follow this up, but I was tired of wasting time and his procrastination. I begrudgingly wrote a list of vacant units within his price range. I also suggested he find another solicitor so that we could finalise the financial arrangements as well. He called me bossy and controlling, which led to yet another argument. I may be a very organised individual, but no one had ever called me controlling before. I replied by declaring how tiring and exasperating this whole thing had been for me. It was dragging out for way too long. He said his life had been very hard too and I never stopped to consider this. I cried out, 'How could your life be any worse than mine right now?' He angrily shouted, 'I am gay and that is hard because unlike you, people like me are not accepted, we are viewed as freaks.' For a moment, I thought he might say it was hard because our marriage broke down or that he would miss the kids and our lifestyle. I should never have expected anything more than that!

The Christmas period was stressful to say the least. Putting up the tree was one hell of an emotional ride. The traditional decorations, baubles and stockings with our names on them, memories with every decoration reminding me of every year that had passed. There were baubles with photos of the kids when they were younger and some old ones that belonged to Julian or myself. I felt the warm tears rolling down my cheeks, as I could no longer see what I was doing. My sister, Grace and her husband Russell, turned up at the front door. She helped me finish the tree, telling me that it was time to start new traditions. She looked like my dear mum and it was now that I realised how much I needed my eldest sister's love and support more than ever. I was very grateful to her and my other three sisters for checking up on me regularly in the next few months.

CHAPTER 14

It was early December and I added a week of long service leave onto my usual Christmas leave so that I could go to Queensland with the two girls. We stayed in a cheap hotel right in the centre of Surfer's Paradise, but it was the best holiday I could ever remember. We made the most of every minute, swimming at the beautiful local beaches, going on rides at the theme parks and the late-night walks around the shopping precinct that was open most of the night. My daughters were great company; I was so proud of the smart, confident young women they were now. It was during this time that I truly discovered who I was, not as a wife or a mother. I realised how much energy I had and how I needed to go out, dance or whatever else I wanted to do. I could enrol at the gym, writing classes, maybe even try singing. The sky was the limit and I was not going to stop until I reached it.

Julian was happy to see us all back home. There was only one more week until Christmas and the paperwork had still not been finalised for the Legal Binding Agreement. He finally made the appointment with his solicitor so he could review the agreement that my solicitor had drawn up. I waited patiently in the carpark as Julian left the solicitor's office, feeling relieved that this would be over, and it would mean that the kids and I would thankfully not lose the family home. I asked him when he thought it would be finalised and sent to my solicitor. As I drove away from the kerb, Julian appeared very quiet and slightly nervous, so I asked the question again. He hesitated for a few minutes and then stuttered as he said, 'The solicitor did not sign the agreement because he advised me against it.' I was astounded to put it mildly. The least he could do for the kids and I after all that he had put us through was make sure that we were secure. I never asked for any of this! The kids certainly played no part in the separation. Throughout the marriage I remained faithful, honest and had dedicated a big chunk of my life. He chose to keep this deep, dark secret, one that destroyed our marriage and harmed us all. He chose to please his mother, scared that she would disown or even shame him. I could feel the blood rushing to my face, my hands gripped tighter at the wheel. I rushed home, bolted to my bedroom and slammed the door shut. The pillow got a fair beating, afraid that I may hit something or someone else with worse consequences. How could I ever trust him again? Does he ever tell the truth? Is he that selfish that even his children are not worth a second thought?

I spoke to Rosie on the phone, barely able to speak over the rush of tears that soaked my face. Rosie advised me that if Julian kept acting in this selfish manner, he would eventually lose everyone, including his children. We were the unfortunate products of a lifetime of lies, the innocent victims whose futures were changed forever. Why should we be forced to sell the house, our home of 15 years? When would there be any light at the end of this dark, dreary tunnel? A promise was made to look after our wellbeing, and it was all just falling apart. I did not want the house just for myself. Our adult kids were still at university and in no hurry to move out of home. I intended to have a will written up to provide for them if anything happened to me, never wanting any future spouse to make a claim on the house. Surely, Julian knew me well enough to know that I am not a selfish person, I have never lied to him. Maybe he can't trust me because he is untrustworthy himself?

If I never had children, I would have suggested a

50-50 split of our assets, which would result in the sale of the house. Who is this stranger? I was hoping he would change his mind and sign the agreement. I could not force his hand, but I knew that if he did not change his mind, I would lose the last ounce of respect that I had for him. I never thought he would act in this way, the man I loved and married had died as far as I was concerned.

In the next few days, I did my best to discuss my issues with Julian. The kids also heard what was happening and told him they were confused as to why he changed his mind. Julian told Sarah that he had every intention of signing the papers, but he was advised by his solicitor to take time to think about it first. Sarah explained to her Dad that he really should have told me of his intentions and reasons, because it has caused me tremendous stress. Later that evening, he spoke to me about everything and promised that he would see his solicitor the following week.

At the end of the week, he handed me a large yellow envelope, announcing that his solicitor informed him that he could get more if he went to court. I stared at him blankly and said, 'Thank-you.' I then reminded him that if we went to court and split everything, the house would definitely have to be sold and the kids and I would have to settle for a tiny unit or even rent a place. He said he never ever wanted us to sell the family home. I read the agreement, it stated that Julian had five years to transfer the house and associated mortgage into my name. I checked that it was signed and put it away in my file.

It was almost Christmas, the first one since the separation. Maree came over from interstate with her husband, Peter, to stay with us for ten days. Normally, I would have the house looking very tidy and smelling like roses, but I was not in any mood for visitors. When she asked me how I was coping, I just burst into tears. I thought I was coping very well, but I realised I was just bottling up my emotions, a culmination of frustration, grief and thinking about the upcoming separation. I felt on edge most of the time, especially on Christmas day. Extra guests turned up unexpectedly early, before I had prepared the special lunch. I retreated to my room, closing the door behind me to take some very deep breaths. To add fuel to the fire, my laptop suddenly stopped working. Everything was going wrong! I just wanted to jump in the car and take off somewhere far away. This would possibly be one of the last Christmases spent together at the house as a family. I could not stop myself from thinking of the fact that I would miss him when he left. I would miss the traditions of Julian making the pudding and cutting the turkey. I would miss our visits to the beach on those hot Summer nights. We used to say that it would be amazing to retire and move to Williamstown. I lay on my bed for another half an hour before coming out to continue with the cooking. We had a lovely meal, exchanged beautiful gifts, but I still felt as if I was at a funeral.

Boxing Day followed and I decided to try my best to look for the positives in the day. The quietness of the day gave us a chance to speak about our feelings and how hard it was to get through the festive season. He embraced me in bed that night, promising to always be friends. No one was ever going to ruin this friendship. Although the cuddle was only brief, it felt soothing to be held, loved and cared for. My emotions had been held in so tightly, I felt like I could burst.

This peace lasted a short time, as argument after argument followed in the ensuing days. We disagreed on a suitable dress for Charlotte to wear at her eighteenth birthday party. The dress was tight fitting and low cut and I worried what others might think. Julian believed it was fine, making a significant point that it was her choice and that she could speak up for herself if anyone commented. I knew she was confident, strong and independent but that was irrelevant. I felt annoyed that Julian did not back me up, feeling like this was just his way of enforcing his opinions on being allowed to be different. He spoke about people making their own mistakes and how people evolve over time. Just another normal conversation that turned into an argument. Julian also brought up the fact that he was controlled by his mother, he could never be true to himself, he could never live as a gay man. I was nothing like his mother.

Every conversation, every situation was brought back to the same issue, his sexuality. I could not control who he was or the breakdown of our marriage. Now I could not even have a normal conversation or express my opinions without it leading to tension and squabbles. This latest fight just made me feel hot and flustered, like steam was coming out of my ears. He would rant for what seemed like hours, hollering that people should not judge others, especially family. I did not have the energy to argue. He told me I was controlling in so many ways. The children should make their own decisions. I snapped, 'Should I let them jump over a bloody cliff if they want to?' He went on to say that I had even controlled him throughout the marriage. I wanted to scream so badly, but it would scare the neighbours. I just sat in silence while the rant went on and on and on. I had never been labelled as controlling in my entire life. He chose to get married, knowing very well that he was gay, and he chose to keep up the charade for over twenty-one years. How dare he call me controlling? I snapped, 'You are a real arsehole and I wish I had never, ever married you in the first place!' Predictably, he asked why I stayed with him if I despised him so much. Julian asked, 'How could you say that you wish you never married me when you earlier said that it was not a total waste?' Well, I did say that because at the time I felt sorry for him and I was also trying to reassure myself that my married life had not been a total failure. I wanted to see the positive in people and situations, hoping many times that the marriage would survive. After discussing my regrets, Julian stood up from the couch, red faced and incensed, yelling in my face, 'I want a man! Don't you get it? I need to finally be who I am, not what everyone else wants me to be!' I stormed out of the room after shouting, 'Piss off then. Just go!' Why was it taking him so long to find a unit? I was stuck between a rock and a hard place. I could not move forward with my life until he left. It felt as though someone was smothering me with a pillow and I was fighting for every breath.

    I sat on my bed, staring at the same old four walls, wondering how I got to this point. I thought deeply about his words, my words and why he spoke to me like this. I once loved him so much and never in a million years did I ever think we would part. He was a stranger, a whole different person to the man I married. I consoled myself by playing music, reminding myself that I never tried to control him. I only made decisions when he could or would not. I often had to be the brave one, the strong one. I remembered one such time when Sarah was accused by a boy of leading her on. His grandmother came to the door, insisting that his study scores were declining because he was on the phone to Sarah all night. Well, Sarah was not interested in him and he was twenty while she was only sixteen. I told the grandmother in no uncertain terms that my daughter was the victim here and she better leave my property before I rang the police. Julian uttered a few words to her, saying he was sorry, and he would talk to Sarah. I was so angry that he did not stand up for Sarah and so was she.

Whenever I showed any sympathy for Julian, he misguidedly took it as a sign that I wanted him to stay. I was so fed up with him telling me he wanted a man. Did he think I was fucking stupid? I made the decision to switch off my emotions. I would not show any sympathy or anger. I would be totally emotionless. He would be invisible to me. I would no longer hug him, smile at him or show any interest in his welfare. He once said it would have been easier if he died. At least then I would have still believed that he loved me. Instead I must grieve my marriage, grieve my husband and then see him daily. How could I avoid him when we still lived under the same roof? I had been and still was a prisoner, trapped in a cell with the enemy. There were moments when I even thought of packing up all his belongings and throwing them out on the lawn, like they do in the movies or that 'Moving Out Today' song by Carol Bayer Sager. I thought of burning all his photos, but I just could not do it.

CHAPTER 15

It had been an entire year since I first read that horrid letter, the one that would change my life and destiny forever. I remember how we initially tried so hard to make the marriage work, truly believing optimistically that with honesty and love it could only get better. I could not have been more wrong. People always said that I let my heart rule my head. All logic was thrown out the window when love was involved. Reading that letter, I focused on one part, 'I hope that you would allow us to continue our marriage journey, albeit a different one.' I once saw a spark of hope that we could just pretend that Julian was straight, and it would all be fine. I was so naïve.

The rest of the Summer was pleasant, long days at the beach as a family, sharing ice-creams and walking bare foot on the sand. Julian had still not secured a place to rent. My sister Maree and her husband went back to Adelaide and we had a lot to do in the coming weeks. Apart from finding a unit, there were finances to sort and belongings to divide up and pack.

The blissful feeling was short-lived once again. A week later we argued about a couple that I knew. The wife was being abused and threatened by her husband and there was a possibility that the husband was gay. Julian was angry that the husband was not getting as much support as the wife, shouting that he could not help who he was. I retaliated, exclaiming that nobody deserves abuse, regardless of the sexuality of the offender. Why did everything have to turn into an argument? Brandon could understand what I was trying to say, and I was grateful for his unbiased and astute perception.

At last, a suitable unit was found, close to public transport and shops and only a ten-minute drive away. There were just a few weeks left until the move and I had no intention of helping with the moving process because it would only trigger emotions that I did not want to show. It was now a reality. My husband of twenty-one years and I would no longer be living together. My status would be changed from married to 'separated', a single mother and eventually even divorced.

When the moving day was only a few days away, I

helped with the last-minute items that needed to be packed. I also helped to organise a budget for Julian because he was extremely stressed about the fact that he may not be able to pay all his bills, whilst still paying the mortgage for the next five years. It was six months since my mother-in-law passed away, so we went to the cemetery. Julian looked miserable, tears running down his gaunt face. The plaque and plastic flowers looked sad and unkempt. As we dusted the flowers and polished the plaque, we both started to cry hysterically, unleashing months of pent up emotion. Tears for a mother who held his secret, who threatened to disown him if he admitted his sexuality. Tears for a woman who loved us both and we would never see again. She would never know that her son could and would now be able to be who he was without her judgement. Both of us had lost our mothers in the last two years and soon we would no longer have our marriage either. We spoke about keeping in touch, offering support to each other and vowing not to date until we healed. I could not even imagine how my life would turn out or if I could ever fall in love again.

 I caught up with my Straight Spouse group in the city, but I was only there physically. I was not sure whether it was the hot weather or my lack of sleep, but I was exhausted and drained. I could not enjoy anything, walking around the house like a zombie, feeling like someone had died. My mood changed from sombre to anger, back to sombre and even erratic. You could cut the tension with a knife as the last few days ensued. Wardrobes and cupboards were cleaned, photos were taken down, a feeling of emptiness engulfed us all.

    I did what I always did when I felt strong emotions, I wrote. I wrote down my thoughts, my fears and wrote a song that expressed my inner emotions.

It seemed so perfect, the fairy tale couple
So much in love, married with kids
White picket fence and a comfortable home
Who would have thought it would be torn up in shreds?

You were my Romeo, a true gentleman
Some people called you soft, I called you kind
Supposed to be forever, my very best friend
Everything changed, how could I be so blind

I was living the dream, you were living a lie
The closet fell open wide, I wanted to cry
I loved you, I needed you but instead you chose him

No longer a family, now on my own
I don't know who I am anymore, you changed my destiny
Dreams destroyed, broken hearts
Collateral damage just to please society

CHAPTER 15

Be your true self, love who you want
Was it worth destroying others to lie and hide?
Sleepless nights, used as a cover and now I'm confused
Loneliness, despair on a long bumpy ride

I was living the dream, you were living a lie
The closet fell wide open, I wanted to cry
I loved you, I needed you but instead you chose him

That week Julian bought me a cute little pot plant, identical to the one he had bought himself for his new place. He packed more of his belongings as I watched on, finally feeling at ease, peaceful even, accepting of what was happening. It was not until familiar love songs played on the radio that my mood changed, and I felt like crying. Singers like Elton John and Ronan Keating just reminded me of times that had past and would never be again.

A large removal truck arrived in our quiet little court, its engine roaring like a bull in a china shop. Piece by piece, the carport was emptied of all the furniture that had sat there covered for months. Brandon, Julian and I followed behind the truck to Julian's flat with the smaller items. I could not go inside the flat. We waved goodbye and I could see him watching in the rear vision mirror as I drove off. Brandon and I headed to the city to have dinner and play minigolf. My heart was racing as I struggled to hold back the tears. I must have cried a river that night. I cried during mini-golf. I cried during dinner. I cried on the long drive home. Brandon looked at me with a sorrowful face, asking if I wanted him to drive instead. I said I would be alright, calming down for only a few minutes before starting all over again. I was so grateful that he was with me, supporting me, hugging me and handing me tissues. He asked me how I was every ten minutes or so, knowing his mother too well. I could never fool him. He was my crutch and my rock. This wonderful son of mine, who I had nurtured for over twenty years was now nurturing me. I was so proud of him, his maturity, caring nature and fervent empathy. When we returned home, Sarah was also feeling miserable that her Dad would no longer be living with us. Together we all hugged and cried. Julian texted us, he was also crying in his tiny flat. The time had arrived, our separation was final, and it was just as tough as I had imagined it to be. No radio tonight. No love songs. I needed to avoid anything that would trigger a flood of tears. I missed my walking buddy. I missed my green tea buddy. I told myself that I deserved more, just as Julian always told me. I still loved him in a way, although I did not want to admit it. It was like when a loved one dies; the love remains as if they are still alive. It wasn't the perfect marriage, not by a long shot but I still cared for his well-being and missed him. It was hard for both of us to let go. A few days later we had dinner in the city together, greeting each other with a hug. We saw each other for three consecutive days. I needed some time to process everything, to get used to being on my own. I got through the nights in the huge bed by myself. It was still Summer, so the room was warm, the scented candles relaxed me as I slept. I could smell a hint of aftershave on the pillow and it was comforting. I found that by placing a cushion on either side helped me to sleep like a baby wrapped in a blanket.

CHAPTER 16

Several days later, I went for a long walk to the local shopping centre on my own. It felt as though a large weight had been lifted from my shoulders. I could finally be myself, focus on my wants and needs. With every step I took, I was letting go of negativity. The fear of Julian cheating... the laptop... the paranoia. I was as free as a bird, feeling as light as a feather as the wind brushed my hair and I could finally breathe naturally once again.

The holidays had ended, and it was time to go back to work for a new school year. I felt exhausted at times, finding it hard to sleep and settle into work when I was coming home to an empty house. The morning routine was different, and I wondered if he was feeling the same way. It did get easier each day and I was grateful for the support I received from the kids and my family. My sisters texted me regularly to check in. Life was busy, I worked long hours, came home to do housework and fitted in a bit of yoga, that I managed to start up again. But my life was finally authentic. I had hopes, dreams and the chance to rediscover who I was as an individual, not as a wife or mother. I now had the chance to study, learn new things, work on my health and just enjoy life. I was free from the internal stress that was so much part of my life for a long time, but I needed time before I started dating again. I needed time to grow, thrive and be that person I always wanted to be. I was fifty years old and my life was beginning all over again. I felt excited.

My disruptive, chaotic childhood had a profound effect on my self-esteem and my ability to fulfil my dreams. My confidence had taken a beating over the years, taking ever and a day to realise that it didn't matter what others thought. I always felt as though I was one person on the inside and the complete opposite on the outside. I appeared quiet and reserved, but on the inside, I wanted to shout, 'This is not me; I want to dance and sing and achieve more in my life.' I just did not have the confidence to do it. My counsellor encouraged me to take risks and to defend myself. It got easier over time.

Two months after Julian moved out, he came over

on alternate weekends to do some gardening and have some pasta with us all. We went for a nice walk like we used to after dinner and had a coffee at the local McDonalds. It was so lovely, being able to communicate without arguing and not have any expectations. I told him I was coping a lot better, focusing on keeping healthy, the kids and my writing. He wanted to date guys one day, but he wasn't ready yet. To a certain extent, I thought I still had some unresolved feelings under the surface, but it had only been a few months, so it was understandable. Julian told me over coffee that he did not want to be promiscuous, philandering around with several men night after night. He wanted just one man in his life for company, someone he could communicate well with who had similar life goals and interests like gardening and art. He had tears in his eyes as he said that the whole separation had been extremely painful and ten years ago he never imagined we would not be together forever. I told him there was just no other way. At least now we did not have the angst, the frustration and resentment towards each other. Strangely we missed each other's company. There were happy times once upon a time and I felt incredibly sad every time I thought of those earlier times. I remembered when we had our first Christmas with Brandon as a baby. I still had the video in my cabinet, one where we played Christmas carols and took turns holding our tiny baby. We could not have been prouder.

I kept my emotions under control most of the time, but then they would erupt unexpectedly at the drop of a hat. While I was at work, keeping busy cleaning the house or talking to others I was fine. As soon as it was quiet, I just felt like hollering, 'I am so lonely, so sad, can I please be transported to a better place, anywhere but here?' Writing down my thoughts was the only way to release the deep-seated tension I felt, even more than walking and yoga. I wondered whether my story could ever be helpful to other women in a similar situation. Could it prevent young men from making a similar mistake?

Music was both soothing and triggering. I have always loved music and dancing. Whenever I felt triggered by a song from the 1990s because it reminded me of my marriage, I would tell myself that I was authentic in my feelings and I had a right to feel despondent. I once loved Julian with all my heart, and I put a lot of sweat and tears into making the marriage work. He never felt the same type of love. He once said I was like a best friend, but one that he enjoyed snuggling up with. I had to stop going over this in my head, it was time to discover who I was again and plan a new future as a single woman.

The loneliness on the weekends was getting harder as

the months went by. I thought about calling friends but most of them had partners and were likely to be either out or spending time with their family. I don't want to be the 'third wheel,' tagging along with a happy couple. I felt sorry for myself, frustrated that I had wasted so many years, persevering in a sexless marriage. How could other people have such successful, long lasting relationships? My eldest sister and her husband have been married for forty-five years and they still act like young lovers. They never turn up to events alone or wonder who they will spend time with on the weekends. I want that kind of love. Last night all three kids were out, and I felt especially lonely, not quite tired enough to sleep but not motivated to call anyone or go out. I opened my refurbished laptop to check my Facebook when an advertisement was staring at me in the face. Speed dating in Melbourne for over forties. I registered, filled out the pages of details but hesitated to press the last button. How could I hit submit? What if I was too intimidated to show up on the night? I guess I could wait and see how I feel at the time. My hand shook over the mouse pad, as the cursor hovered over that dreaded word. I took a deep breath and hit the button without looking. What did I have to lose? I think I was ready to start dating or at least meet people and it was never going to happen if I sat at home every night. If only Prince Charming could appear on my door step one day!

Julian and I remained amicable over the next few months, catching up for coffee every now and then or he would have dinner with the kids and me. We greeted each other with a hug, but he broke away quite quickly. When he asked if I wanted to go to the Art Gallery the following week, I told him I was too busy. It was true, but I wanted to create some distance between us for fear of spending too much time together. Life was busy, work was full on, aside from the domestic chores and other family commitments. Celebrations came and went, including Valentine's Day. The kids knew it would be distressing for me, so they bought me chocolates, flowers and perfume. I felt so blessed to have these beautiful children that had grown into the most caring, thoughtful young adults. I thought back to previous Valentine's Days, cards with writing. Words, words and more words. Meaningless words. I decided not to dwell too much, to finally let go. My future was looking brighter and that was my focus from now on.

I wanted to find love, if that was at all possible. After all, I was almost fifty-one years old. Were there even any decent, single men left in my age range? If I could not find love, I was hoping to at least receive some affection. It would be beautiful to have someone to kiss, hold me and really want me. Someone who would think of me when they made love. But I needed to love myself first, concentrate on my physical and mental health. There were times when I still felt a little angry and traumatised, that is when I would go to the shed and exercise to let out my pent-up anger.

CHAPTER 17

The speed dating evening had arrived. I arrived twenty minutes early, wearing my new navy-blue dress and high heels. I sat at the small table with my diet coke, trying desperately to stop my knees from shaking. When the over enthusiastic host came to the room, he asked the women to take a seat at one of the small square tables. Slowly, one-by-one, the men came into the room sitting opposite the women. The first man that sat opposite me was very short, bald with a moustache. He looked me over like I was for sale. I shook his hand and tried to make a conversation, but he only wanted to talk about his dog, camping and fishing. I felt myself zoning out but smiled and nodded at the appropriate times. The next guy was very attractive and well groomed, almost feminine. Did he turn up to the right speed dating? He was funny, but there was no way I was going there again. The next ten came and went. I only ticked one man, Bob. He seemed interesting and down to Earth so I thought I should at least try to have a second date, or it would be a waste of a night.

Over the next few weeks, Bob and I texted each other. He had custody of his three children and appeared to be a very caring, responsible person. We had coffee at a local café. I was so nervous and found that I was not attracted to him at all. There was no spark for me. His eyes did not leave me over the next hour. He even asked the waitress, 'Could I please have a cappuccino for my lady?' I was not anybody's lady. He then told me I was the 'whole package.' He could not wait to take me camping and for me to meet his children. It was all moving too fast. Although it was nice to know that a man could find me attractive and want me to be a part of his life, I could not imagine ever being intimate with him. When we left, I apprehensively agreed to call him. I walked briskly to the carpark and sat in the car for what seemed like hours. I felt sick to the stomach. I could never see him more than a friend, yet he already envisioned a future with me. Over the next week, I dreaded telling him the truth, fearful of his reaction. Of course, I wanted to be loved, adored and cherished, but I needed to feel the same way. In the end, I texted him, stating that he was a great person, but I was just not ready to move on. He was very gracious, telling me that I was beautiful on the inside and outside. How reassuring that was to hear.

On the weekend, the family got together for coffee. Julian and I agreed that our relationship problems were very similar. He also knew a man in his drama course that showed interest in him, but he was far from his type of man. We knew we would remain friends, being able to discuss anything when we were not in a relationship and there would never be any expectations.

My life was so much better. I started tutoring to earn more money and this paid for my swimming lessons and socialising. I continued to talk with people in the Straight Spouse group and they gave lots of sound advice. Boundaries with Julian were put in place, so we did not take our friendship further and I started referring to him as the children's father rather than my ex. As my wedding anniversary approached, I kept positive, booking in a relaxing massage for the day. I was content with life, had an amazing job, a loving family, loyal friends and good health. It did feel as though a heavy burden had been lifted from my shoulders. My confidence levels had risen immensely, and life was bloody good. The house also felt more peaceful, especially now that we had our cat, Sapphire, there to entertain us. He enhanced all our lives; we were all happier knowing he was part of our family.

The kids had a better relationship with their father than they ever did when he was living at home. No more misunderstandings or angry outbursts. Sarah did not always have a positive relationship with her Dad when he lived with us, as he always took life so seriously. Brandon confided in me, explaining that he always felt uneasy during discussions with his Dad about many things, especially about helping around the home or looking for work. I always found that it was better to focus on the positives when it came to the children, especially the older two as they suffered from anxiety. Sometimes I got it wrong, particularly when I was stressed myself, and I always felt horrible after an argument. The home should be a retreat from stress after all the pain we experience in other parts of our lives, whether it was work, money or health. I feel myself smile widely when I see how we are all thriving. I am a proud mother.

Julian and I maintained our harmonious friendship, catching up over the occasional meal, or after lending a hand with the garden or chopping wood. We had established our boundaries, hugs, no kisses, and we both had a new respect for each other. This may change slightly after one of us has a partner, but that has not happened yet. I was still part of the Straight Spouse group, surprised at how many new members there were daily. Even in 2017, there were still so many

CHAPTER 17

people living a lie in their relationship, frightened to be found out or wanting the best of both worlds. I am grateful to be further along in my journey, but sometimes have flashbacks when I hear of others who are suffering the anguish that I once did. There was just no time in my life to regret my past and reminisce. I will say one thing though. I never really felt like it was a proper marriage in the first place. How much was real? What part was make-believe, a sham? Many of the last twenty-two years of my life were based on lies and keeping the peace. It was as though I was holding my breath under water for most of the time. However, my life now was real. I could feel, taste and live the peaceful life that I always craved for.

As the year progressed and life just got busier with work, housework, tutoring and paying bills, I felt quite overwhelmed. I felt myself burning out, as I did everything from washing, ironing, cooking, cleaning and even chopping wood. One day, I just exploded and broke down in tears, informing the kids that I needed more help before I became ill. There were times when I wanted to swap roles with Julian so he would know what it was like to be a single-parent. He did not take this very well. I ultimately wrote up a roster for the kids and I so we could share the load amongst the four of us. That weekend, I went to Adelaide with Brandon for a few days to watch the footy and to visit my sister,

Maree. Julian stayed with the girls, texting regularly to let me know that everything was going well, and he tidied the house. I missed his precious help around the house, he was even fussier than me at times. I thanked him and he replied that he wished 'the best of everything for me.' It was nice.

When I returned home, I took up Latino dancing, learning a few moves, although I would never be Beyoncé, more like her mother. It was lovely though to mix with others, doing something exciting and feeling a sense of freedom that I had not experienced for some time. I continued dancing for a few months, stopping when I got a nasty head cold. My whole body was aching, and it took a little while to feel healthy and fit again. I lay there at night really wishing that I could find a partner, someone that would love me as much as I could love them. I was too scared to go online to search but maybe one day I would venture into the online dating world.

CHAPTER 18

The gay marriage debate continued in Parliament as well as in the general community. There was no escape. It was so hard to bear at times because it triggered so many feelings that I had buried. Watching old family videos were also not easy to view without some sadness, but life was just different and better in many ways. Elton John apologised to his ex-wife Renate, whom he had married in Australia. He encouraged Australians to vote yes for gay marriage, stating that he loved and admired Renate but he denied who he really was, causing sadness to her and guilt and regret for himself. The story was familiar and all too common.

During this time, I attended my dearest uncle's funeral in New South Wales. He was my mum's youngest brother, the youngest of thirteen children.

I travelled over with my sisters and their husbands. During the funeral, my three sisters sat next to their partners, hand in hand, a shoulder to cry on. I sat by myself. I wished that I had a man next to me, someone who cared deeply for me, who would hand me their handkerchief and kiss away my tears. It was hard to sit there wiping my own tears, sad for Uncle Don and sad for my loneliness. After the funeral, we went to a local pub for a meal. The feeling of isolation only continued after all the husbands got up to pay for their partners' meals and get them drinks, while I joined them, paying for my own meal. It was not about the money; it was just the lack of love in my life. I quietly stared into space with a smile on my face, coercing myself to snap out of this self-pity.

As the weeks and months progressed, many of my friends and family spoke of guys that they knew who I could date, but none of them appealed to me. That was until a friend from my Straight Group, Janny, suggested that I meet her friend, Charlie. She apparently showed him a photo of me weeks earlier and he responded that I 'was lovely.' I reluctantly asked to see a photo of him, so she immediately sent one through to my mobile. I replied that he looked very handsome and friendly. A few weeks went by and I thought no more of it until Janny mentioned him again. I was curious to know more about him. He had lovely hair,

CHAPTER 18

gorgeous blue eyes with a twinkle that already had me in a trance. He was a year and a half older than me, had been married many years ago but had no children. A Scottish engineer who had lived in Australia for about ten years. Janny asked if I was happy for her to give my mobile number to Charlie. I nervously agreed, thinking I really had nothing to lose by speaking on the phone to a handsome man.

A few days later, Charlie and I began talking for hours every night. He was very easy to talk to, had a gorgeous Scottish accent and an intelligence that I truly craved for in a man. I could not wait to meet him the following weekend. We agreed to meet at a charming café overlooking the river, midway between our two suburbs. As I stepped out of the car, I checked my appearance in the window, applied more lipstick and proceeded across the road to the café. I truly believe that first appearances are so important. I walked over quickly and noticed he was behind the counter with his back facing me. I tried my hardest to appear relaxed as I called his name in case it was someone else. He politely stood up and we greeted each other with a gentle handshake. We faced each other over our coffee, eyes meeting and not leaving each other for the next two hours. I was mesmerised by his dreamy blue eyes, not to mention his sexy Scottish accent. We spoke about everything from family to our favourite ice-cream. I felt so comfortable talking to this handsome, interesting and well-travelled gentleman. His stories were endless and fascinating, and he soon had me eating out of the palm of his hand. He paid the bill and walked me to my car. Just after kissing me on the cheek he asked if I would like a second date. I replied quickly with a smile, 'Of course!'

The next weekend we went to the movies. Charlie reached over and held my hand straight away which made me feel a little uncomfortable, like a teenager on their first ever date. I could feel his eyes on me at the movies and when I gazed up at him he would be smiling from cheek to cheek. After the movie, he walked me to my car, where we jumped in to the back seat to have a cuddle and a passionate kiss. The underground carpark was well lit, so it was no wonder a couple of middle-aged ladies could see us in the car as we kissed and hugged. They rolled their eyes and got in their car, thankfully driving off. We both laughed like teenagers as I felt myself blush with embarrassment, something I had not done for many years. Charlie asked if I would like to go to his unit where we could talk more and feel more relaxed. I followed him back to his place, all the while wondering if I was doing the right thing. I felt excited but nervous at the same time because I had not had proper sex for at least five years. This was so spontaneous for a person who normally must plan and write down everything from shopping lists to what I need to bring to a picnic. Would we have sex? Would it still be the same? What if he thought I was unattractive? As we entered he apologised for the mess and cleared a space on the black leather couch for us both. He gave me that look, reached over and kissed me so passionately that I felt at home in his arms. He took my hand and led me to his room, continuing to kiss and touch me. It felt so exciting to be touched like this after all these years. I felt younger, sexy and closed my eyes to enjoy his hands all over my body. He ran his fingers through my hair and caressed my legs and breasts. I also fondled him, impressed with the hardness of his penis. I was ready. He did not stop until we had both come three times in different positions. I could feel his warmth, his sweat and I relaxed again into his arms. We laid together, snuggling or spooning as they call it now. For a long while, we just talked and kissed before I got dressed to go home, not prepared to stay the whole night.

Over the next few months there were many romantic dinners out at quirky restaurants and cafés. We took turns to sleep over at his house or mine. The kids met Charlie and thought he was funny and could tell that he loved me. We missed each other when we were apart. He would occasionally come over during the week nights after work, bringing flowers and chocolates. We discussed having overseas holidays together some day. My love for Charlie grew each day, knowing he would be there for me whenever I needed him. He was also great with the kids, giving them advice regarding work and other issues they were experiencing.

It felt too good to be true. There were days when I doubted the strength of our relationship at times, feeling stressed and lacking confidence. I saw my counsellor, who helped me understand that I felt unworthy because of my past and the rejection from Julian. It wasn't as though Charlie was unaffectionate towards me, he hardly took his hands off me. He also gave me a copy of keys to his unit, showing his trust, but I needed to learn to trust him as well.

Charlie was a little jealous of my friendship with Julian, even though I explained many times that Julian was gay, and we would never get back together. He often made jokes about Julian always being at my house, but he was only over once a fortnight. He would learn to accept that Julian and I were good friends, nothing more.

There were more outings, to the drive-in movies and dinners. Charlie was so supportive when it came to advice or fixing things around the house, but he was not very tidy. His unit was quite messy and unorganised, cluttered with clothes, papers and bike parts. He did not often give me a hand with the dishes or cleaning up at my place so I could not ever see myself ever living with him. The other thing that frustrated me was his tightness with money. He would only turn on his hot water when he needed to do dishes or have a shower. We had been together for four months and I would wait until another two months before I decided if we were adequately compatible for the long term. I concentrated on the positives and was determined to give it my best shot. We did not even have a song, but maybe one day we will. Julian and I had many songs that reminded us of each other and our first few years together, but none of that matters now. Charlie and I went on a boat cruise from Williamstown to Melbourne. The weather was beautiful and sunny. As we sat on the ferry, we cuddled closely taking photos of the sea and of ourselves. As I relaxed into his strong arms, I felt so loved and could not imagine life without Charlie. I wanted to get my divorce settled, hoping that someday Charlie may propose. He became more helpful at home and I just watched him in awe as he fixed cupboards and the drainpipes outside.

My relationship with Julian improved tenfold as a best friend, my bestie. He was careful not to tread on Charlie's toes, but was always there when I really needed him. One week I had the worst gastro that I had ever experienced, vomiting to no end. Sarah was the only child home and she had a phobia of bodily fluids.

Charlie was not much better. Julian rushed over to clean up after me and pick up my medicines. He also checked up on me when he knew it would be a hard day for me, like the anniversary of Mum's death or other such occasions. At times, he made soup for me and sent it over with the kids. We regularly spent time with the kids as a family, knowing that it meant the world to them and it felt very special. Whether Charlie and I stay together forever or not, I know Julian will always be in my life, as the children's father and as a mate. Where we once argued because of confusion, we now listen with understanding and acceptance.

Three years since that dreaded discovery that my husband was gay, I am in a much better place. One chapter has closed, and another has begun. As I plan for my gorgeous daughter Sarah's twenty-first birthday, I have two amazing but very different men helping me with the setting up and the cooking. One is my lover and my future, and one will always be my best friend. They are not mates or even that close, but they are both important to me. Julian will always be around to celebrate the kids' birthdays, at special festivities like Christmas and Easter. He will be there to listen, a shoulder to cry on, my confidante. But the love of my life is Charlie. There are no guarantees with relationships that it will last forever, but for now at least, I feel truly blessed.

CHAPTER 18

Living a lie (song)

It seemed so perfect, a fairy-tale couple
So much in love, married with kids
White picket fence, a beautiful home
Who ever thought it would be torn up in shreds?

You were my prince, a true gentleman
Some called you soft, but no you were kind
Supposed to be forever. You were my best friend
Things were changing, why was I so blind?

I was living a dream, you were living a lie
The closet was wide open, I wanted to cry
I loved you, I needed you but instead you chose him

No longer a family, now on my own
I don't know who I am anymore, you have changed my destiny
Dreams destroyed, broken hearts
Collateral damage just to please society

Be yourself, love who you want
Was it worth destroying others to lie and hide?
Sleepless nights, used as a cover and now I'm confused
Loneliness, despair, a long bumpy ride.

My Gay Husband

I was living a dream, you were living a lie
The closet was wide open, I wanted to cry
I loved you, I needed you but instead you chose him.

www.ingramcontent.com/pod-product-compliance
Lightning Source LLC
Chambersburg PA
CBHW021106080526
44587CB00010B/411